STORY
C A T E C H I S M

Freddy Williams
David Comstock

STORY catechism

Cover design and layout: 407, www. Fourohseven.com

Scripture quotations are from the ESV ® Bible (The Holy Bible, English Standard Version ®), copyright © 2001 by Crossway. 2011

"In Judaism, the Rabbis were known to come together and wrestle with the difficult parts of the Torah; this is known as . Through Story Catechism we've been given an opportunity to gather collectively as a family and participate in our own midrash of sorts. Freddy Williams has compacted a creative outlet to walk through the narrative of scripture that is simple but not superficial or shallow. He's given us the resource to gather the family around the table and have a conversation about God's relentless pursuit of his creation. This will impact homes for generations to come."

Cody Deese, founder LeadNEXT

Story Catechism is a gift for families, as it presents the truths of Scripture in a memorable, accessible, and gospel-centered way. It is both practical and profound in inviting our children into the story of Scripture as the framework for their life.

Brian Bennett, founder of Multiply Leaders

"Every night when I tuck my three-year-old son into bed, just like clockwork he looks at me and says, "Daddy, tell me a story." Even at three years old, my son's heart is captivated by a story--why? Because we were made for the story... for God's story. What SC allows me to do as a husband and father is reach deep into the story God has written, reach deep into my children's hearts, and by God's grace, merge the two. SC is an invaluable resource for my family and will be for yours, as well."

Jason Jordan, West Side Community Church

"As the parent of 9 children under the age of 12, our family has to fight to make our family worship time productive. Story Catechism has been an immeasurable blessing in this area. It is theologically sound, easy to use, and keeps different-aged children engaged. I highly recommend this resource."

Jeff Neville, Red Tree Churches

"Deep within us, in the region of our soul, there is a longing to know and embrace The Love Story. This longing does not begin at a certain age or stage of development. It is within us from conception, and our soul cries out to know, understand, and simply be part of The Story. SC has given parents, grandparents, or anyone seeking the simplicity of God's Story, another tool in the toolbox. This tool will be invaluable to a generation that must sift through more stories than ever before in search of Truth. In SC, the Love Story of Jesus is clearly, and foundationally, given in a way that is appropriate for any developmental level."

Gary Carter, Journey Church

DEDICATION

To our sons...

Ryder, your passion is sincere; your heart, loyal; your friendship, sweet. You are the heart of our family.

Scout, your curiosity knows no bounds; your laugh brings life; you are fantastically wild. You bring the sunshine.

The Father has used you to reveal the depths of love. Keep sailing.

- Freddy

To our children...

Julia, your unquenchable curiosity and courageous spirit have allowed us to have adventures that will shape our family for generations to come. You are a beautiful gift.

Moses, Your little voice, giant laugh, and precious songs fill our home and our hearts everyday.

You both help us to experience the beautiful rhythms of God's grace.

- David

"CHRISTIANITY IS THE STORY ABOUT HOW THE RIGHTFUL KING HAS LANDED, YOU MIGHT SAY LANDED IN DISGUISE, AND IS CALLING US ALL TO TAKE PART IN A GREAT CAMPAIGN OF SABOTAGE."

C. S. LEWIS
MERE CHRISTIANITY

THANK YOU
from Freddy

My father and mother, Bob and Jeannette. This is about the story of God. Thanks for sharing it with us.

To our families, thank you for your continued love, encouragement, and support.

Kristin White, thanks for being a soldier. Thanks for bringing SC to life.

Kayla Mugler and Ryan Weiss, thanks for sharing in the love of words and making mine make sense.

Tim Blankenship, thanks for jumping into the trenches with me. You have broad shoulders and a big heart.

David Comstock, your friendship runs deep; thanks for believing in this.

Ekklesia, your courage continues to inspire me. Keep going. Forge ahead.

Lastly, to my best friend, my bride, my love, Michele Williams. You fill my heart, you fill my head, you keep me grounded. You overwhelm me. You make me smile. You are both home and adventure.

You are still my muse.

THANK YOU
from David

Jesus for the sweet gift of life. You have rescued me from my sin and invited me to participate in a life I never thought possible. Thank you, thank you, thank you.

Mom and John, for teaching me about the beauty of generosity and the power of hospitality. You have always made room in your life for anyone and everyone. Thank you for your witness.

Jeff Neville, Thank you for teaching me to take risks and trust in truth. Your family has been a blessing to ours.

To our Gospel Community for teaching us the beauty of transparency in the midst of family.

"Smitty" - Your friendship and trust continues to humble me. Thank you for taking risks with me and stepping out in faith when my ideas sound crazy.

Mid-Cities, you have no idea what a blessing you have been in my journey to discover the power of God and the beauty of each one of our voices as we lift up the name of Christ.

Finally, To the one who is a daily reminder of God's steadfast grace and covenantal love, my daily joy, my best friend, my anchor. Tara Comstock you have inspired me in ways that you will never know. Your friendship has become my greatest place of rest and my greatest source of motivation. Your beauty captures my heart more and more everyday.

FOREWORD

Walking into a tent in rural Western New York, my brother-in-law introduced me, "This is Freddy, the student I told you about." It was obvious even as a senior in high school that Freddy Williams was going to spend his life leading people.

Five years later I hired this confident yet teachable young man and his young bride to join our team serving students in St. Charles, Missouri. I had the privilege of watching Freddy love and serve teenagers and then go on to plant a church, listening to the stories of anyone who happened across his path. It seems to me that the truly great leaders are those who have learned to listen. If you have ever had "a coffee" with this young pastor, you know what it feels like to be heard, valued, and known.

Freddy has an enthusiasm that is boundless. Yet somehow, he has harnessed that enthusiasm and channeled it into a robust narrative called Story Catechism. I have already experienced this treasure of insight being quoted back to me from my youngest daughter. It infuses my heart with joy listening to my child articulate the love of God and the great mission of Jesus.

It has been sixteen years since I first met the young student under the tent that was sure to be a leader. He now leads me.

Jamie George
Franklin, Tennessee
Author and Pastor of The Journey Church

IF WE DON'T CONNECT THE DOTS FOR OUR CHILDREN, THEN SOME OTHER NARRATIVE WILL.

STORY CATECHISM

THE JOURNEY

*"The Christian ideal has not been tried and found wanting;
it has been found difficult and left untried."*
G. K. Chesterton [1]

This is a story; it's a brilliant story, because it's a real story with real implications. It's a story about a valiant hero and a defeated villain. It's a story that pierces the heart with untold beauty and bottomless pain, where perfection collides with pride and a battle for the heart of the beloved ensues.

Some stories are real.

This is one of them.

In the west, the family as we know it is disintegrating. Though it was once the center of the human experience, the family seems more like a relic of the past, a rumor of what used to be. The idyllic dream of raising a family seems crushed beneath the weight of what this world has to offer. We live in a world that is both beautiful and dark; a dissonance of experience; a juxtaposition of beliefs; an ever-changing, ever-expanding matrix of diversity. Racial tension, corrupt governments, impeding corporations, imminent warfare, waning resources, increasingly unrealistic expectations, all in an over-stimulated, over-sexualized culture.

Perhaps many of us feel like raising a family is impossible.

Raising our families in the way of the gospel is not only possible--but it's commanded, and empowered through the work of the Holy Spirit. This is not just another task to perform in our already crushing and over-committed lifestyles. This is one of the highest callings and most profound invitations ever given. The grand design of love was created to be experienced in the context of grace-filled, loving family.

Do you ever find yourself asking, "God, are you sure... me? You know me. Us? C'mon, really? You want us to raise these children?" With the weight of responsibility, the daunting task of discipleship, and the overwhelming void of "know-how," where do we even begin?

Ask Google about parenting advice, and 140,000,000 options emerge in 0.36 seconds. Search Amazon for parenting resources and you'll find 90,000 books to ferret through. Or better yet, tune in to listen to all the latest suggestions by the "experts" on the morning and afternoon talk shows. Not to mention, many of our churches are running glorified daycares. In the event that we actually find something we like, it seems that a one-size-fits-all approach actually, well--fits no one. Our children are each beautifully unique and wonderfully individual. Of my (Freddy) two boys, one loves defined boundaries while the other plays hopscotch with them. One is cautious, the other is slightly reckless. One is over-the-top observant, and the other, I have to incessantly remind to, pay attention. One likes to blame; the other immediately hides. One is a vibrant thrill-seeker, the other, though insatiably curious, is quite calculated. They are raised by the same parents in the same family with the same surroundings, yet these boys are entirely unique. There are no formulas to parenting, no paint-by-the-numbers kits for raising children. There are no laboratories for love.

No one ever told me how difficult it would be to pastor and disciple my own family. As a husband and a daddy of two boys, I have felt more insecurity and trepidation in the midst of my clear inadequacy to disciple and lead my family in worship than I have in any other relationship. I have been a full-time pastor for over a decade, and it seems the most difficult and profound call on my life has been the shepherding and discipleship of my family. With the resurrection of conversation and the resurgence of family worship, I felt shame in my failed attempts to lead my family in this arena.

I wasn't raised in a family or church community that practiced family worship. Family worship is simply a time set aside for your family to gather and worship in the home. Though the idea wasn't foreign to me, it was not practiced—maybe just forgotten. It seems my wife and I learn through much trial and mostly error. We planted a church made of many young families learning how to become families, the majority of which were birthed out of their own dysfunctional and broken experiences. We needed a new way forward. Our family discovered the beautiful depth and invitation of story.

Story possesses invitation, a way forward that invites pilgrimage into the complexity. A path that leads into more questions and life-giving conversation, not just short, pithy rhetoric that fits on a t-shirt or a bumper sticker. It's beyond maxims and anecdotes, beyond trite sayings and easy pat answers. Formulas and clichés cannot arrest the affections of the heart. The way forward is through invitation. Story invites us, beckons us, and woos us. It's the language of the heart and an interpreter of the soul. Story, the recounting of a sequence of events, has been a formative way of understanding and learning throughout history. Story has a way of revealing to the human soul something deeper than information, something more than knowledge. Story has a way of creating a bridge between the soul and the mind; a way of creating passage between the turbulent waters and the places of refuge, a passage between the brokenness of the human experience and the fullness of being human. Story creates sanctuary.

We created STORY catechism (SC) with the desire and intent to begin a conversation that invites our families into life's deeper echo; the sweeping metanarrative of our story. It's an invitation to cultivate and learn, to teach and journey into the greatest story ever told, and find our place in it.

We are hopeful and prayerful that our children will invite us into their questions and struggles. That grace would mark our homes and a genuine humility would saturate our hearts. Grace gives us awareness to experience the depth of our need. Grace stirs the deep waters of our hearts and gives us the opportunity to stir the deep waters of our children's hearts. It reminds us there is more. There is more beyond what our hands can produce, more beyond our achievements and our failures. In the Sacred Romance, Brent Curtis and John Eldredge write, "If we aren't aware of our soul's deep thirst, His offer means nothing." [2] Our souls are thirsty, our desperation ever-present. We are learning daily how badly we need help, just how desperate we are for wisdom and guidance.

His offer means everything.

The pilgrimage ahead was written to engage our hearts and minds. The desire is that these words begin to expand our understanding and insight and begin to lay the bedrock in our families' stories. May these words awaken us from our slumber and draw us into something more. May we find freedom and invitation in the biblical narrative. May we learn from the perfect Father and the perfect Son, guided by the Holy Spirit.

Perhaps A. W. Tozer said it best in The Knowledge of the Holy when he wrote, "While I believe that nothing will be found here contrary to sound Christian theology, I yet write not for professional theologians but for plain persons whose hearts stir them up to seek after God Himself." [3]

As plain persons and fellow sojourners, we would like to extend an invitation to stay awhile, to take a deep rest, to journey together and to explore the biblical narrative as a family. We are not experts in this arena, just men and women acutely aware of our desperation.

This is Story Catechism.

INSTRUCTIONS

Train up a child in the way he should go; even when he is old he will not depart from it.
Proverbs 22v6

Children are a heritage from the LORD, offspring a reward from him.
Psalm 127v3

The purpose in a man's heart is like deep water, but a man of understanding will draw it out.
Proverbs 20v5

On the journey of parenting, we have this beautiful privilege of guiding our children to the places of understanding. Genuine understanding is rooted deep within the heart and the mind. The gospel finds its home there; in the innermost depths of who we are, truth rests. This truth grows into the beautiful garden of identity. The deep waters of our children's hearts must be reached if the seed of understanding is to take root.

The psalmist writes, "Our children are a heritage, a blessing" (Psalm 127v3), so the great obstacle, in our busy, over-committed, and always-on lifestyles, is to not simply remain on the edges and only navigate the circumference. We are consumed by the circumference of our lives. The western veneer hides the depth of our neediness and only further feeds our pride and entrenches our hearts in fear. But we have been invited into more; the call of Jesus invites us to actively embrace the responsibility to move from the edges of our children's world, to the center of their hearts. This is precisely the invitation of the gospel. Jesus constantly meets us in our unbelief and beckons us back.

> *"Thirsty hearts are those whose longings have been wakened by the touch of God within them."*
> **A.W. Tozer**[1]

If we are going to train our children up in the way of the gospel, we must be able to move toward their hearts. If we never move toward their hearts, life will naturally shift externally; life will tend to revert to performance and expectation. Our hope and desire of STORY catechism is to invite our families to develop new rhythms that help overcome the cultural obstacles we face.

SC RHYTHM
There is a simple rhythm designed to help move our families through SC; read, memorize, chat, and pray. Every time we gather for family worship, we read scripture, memorize *Story Catechism*, chat about the journey, and end with a prayer written specially for each section.

READ
Over 90,000 books on Amazon... Over 140,000,000 options on parenting advice on Google... Where do we begin? There is great wisdom from great resources; we want to start with the Bible. While we believe there are great resources available, we believe the Bible is the most trustworthy source that exists.

> *"The Bible is not an end in itself, but a means to bring men to an intimate and satisfying knowledge of God, that they may enter into Him, that they may delight in His presence, may taste and know the inner sweetness of the very God Himself in the core and center of their hearts."*
> **A.W. Tozer**[2]

Hear, O Israel: The LORD our God, the LORD is one. Love the LORD your God with all your heart and with all your soul and with all your strength. These commandments that I give you today are to be on your hearts. Impress them on your children. Talk about them when you sit at home and when you walk along the road, when you lie down and when you get up. Tie them as symbols on your hands and bind them on your foreheads. Write them on the doorframes of your houses and on your gates.

Deuteronomy 6v4-9

All Scripture is breathed out by God and profitable for teaching, for reproof, for correction, and for training in righteousness.
2 Timothy 3v16

We have included a few hundred passages of scripture that your family will ultimately go through when journeying in SC. Every family is unique and every dynamic different. You will discover how many passages make the most sense for your family to go through at any given time. We've noticed that for our family, one passage of scripture at a time is most beautiful. As you travel along, you'll find what is best for your family.

NOTE: All scripture included in SC is in the ESV.

MEMORIZE

We never set out to write a catechism. Quite honestly, when we embarked on the journey of family worship, we didn't even know what a catechism was or what it meant to catechize our children. We set out to engage more with our children and develop deeper conversation about things that matter. We found that the cadence of questions and answers began to produce understanding at a very young age. We learned that the back-and-forth rhythm of questions and answers is extremely powerful when applied to narrative. The minds and hearts of our children are beautiful. Their imaginations are fantastically wild. As parents we need to learn how to have conversation that invites their beautifully wild hearts and minds into the wildly untamed story of God. It's the story their hearts were created to know; a sweeping narrative designed to invite them to discover. It's the story we find ourselves in. The adventure pursues us and invitation lies ahead. May we as parents engage and allow the story to stir the deep waters of our families' hearts.

Keep my commandments and live; keep my teaching as the apple of your eye; bind them on your fingers; write them on the tablet of your heart.
Proverbs 7v2-3

Catechism (kat-i-kiz-uhm) is defined as a summary of the principles of Christian religion in the form of questions and answers, used for the instruction of Christians. Simply put, it's the cadence of questions and answers for the purpose of creating understanding. For centuries, the Christian Church has used the method and journey of catechesis to have deeper conversation about God, the church, theology, doctrines, etc. Sadly, we've come to find that many Christian families think it is the church's task and responsibility to raise their children in the ways of the gospel, yet the Bible is clear on the role of parents raising their children in ways of the gospel. The author of proverbs writes, "Train up a child in the way he should go; even when he is old he will not depart from it" (Proverbs 22v6).

Why *Story Catechism*? Unlike a traditional catechism, in which there are defined and clear questions and answers, SC moves like a narrative. Thus, Story Catechism. In place of memorizing maxims and anecdotes, SC seeks to create the opportunity to memorize and engage in story, specifically biblical theology.

Biblical theology is the approach taken from the perspective of understanding the progressive history of God revealing himself to humanity. It particularly seeks to understand how each part ultimately points forward to fulfillment in the life mission of Jesus. Biblical theology is about the glory of Christ on every page.

Why memorize? Humanity was created to experience the depth of the creator's love and to fully engage in His creation. The story of God invites us to fill the deep wells of our hearts with the truth of the scriptures and then learn how to draw from the depth.

I have stored up your word in my heart, that I might not sin against you.
Psalm 119v11

I delight to do your will, O my God; your law is within my heart.
Psalm 40v8

We suggest that your family does not move to the next section of catechism until the current section has been memorized. We also suggest that you include the previous pieces of the catechism in the current section to constantly remind and further embed the story into memory. This helps create the rhythm of *Story Catechism* by consistently hearing narrative. We have included a single page after each section solely dedicated to "seeing" *Story Catechism*. We call this visual catechism. We understand that for many people, visuals can be helpful to committing something into memory.

CHAT

Dialogical conversation is paramount in creating understanding. By chatting with our families, we can watch the ebb and flow of SC take shape. We have noticed that by asking questions, we encourage the process. It's in this processing that understanding takes root. This is where the garden begins to blossom. The conversations we have during our family worship will provide the fodder for the everyday, moment-to-moment conversations that will naturally emerge. *Dialogue gives our children a voice.*

It's in these conversations that we learn how to engage each other. These moments create access to our hearts and minds. This space creates vulnerability and invites us to engage at a greater depth; to wonder and process out loud and begin to connect the dots to see something more beautiful.

Many of us have not been taught the art of conversation. The majority of us have learned through lecture-style classroom modules. Material is taught only to be regurgitated, to show that we have "learned" it. The ability to memorize and parrot a response back does not show that we learned and understand. This is why conversation, the rhythm of back-and-forth, the cadence of questions and answers, invites us into the process of understanding.

The biblical understanding of the word hear carries with it the idea of listening to respond. Not just to respond with words in the moment, but also in life, with action. It connotes listening with an attentive ear. Essentially, listening is never passive; it's not static. We are invited to model what it means to listen as our children have a voice in these conversations. *We might just learn something from them if we listen closely.*

Included in each section are five questions with brief and concise answers. These are pilot questions you can ask each time to seed the conversation ahead. Our family will typically ask one of the provided questions, see where the trajectory of the conversation is headed, and build the dialogue from that starting place. This approach allows room for more questions to be asked later, so we build upon knowledge rather than trying to accomplish everything in one sitting. In most instances, we have learned that less is more. This gives our family the ability to have the long view in mind.

We believe that God reveals who He is through the scriptures. In short, this is called theology. Theology is studying God's character and nature; it's the revelation of who God says He is on His terms. Theology is important. In each section, the first question is always, what did we learn about God? God is always revealing more of who He is and what He is doing. The last question in every section is, where and how do we see the gospel? We believe the glory of Christ is on every page in the scriptures. Jesus is the image of the invisible God, the apostle Paul writes in Colossians (1v15). Through the birth, life, death, and resurrection of Jesus, God the Father is beautifully and fully put on display. We see theology most clearly lived out in the person and work of Jesus. Empowered by the Holy Spirit, may our families vibrantly experience the beautiful and all-sufficient gospel of Jesus Christ.

PRAY

We have a firm conviction that prayer invites and unveils the desperation and longing in our souls. Prayer is the invitation, not to God as a cosmic vending machine, but to God as father. As family—sons and daughters, brothers and sisters—we humbly approach our good and loving father. He has clothed us with worth, bestowed us honor, and invited us as distinguished guests.

Prayer is the posture of submission, the disposition of humility. It is a confession of neediness, a need that is beyond what our hands can supply. Prayer is the posture of confidence with which we commune with the one who has faithfully and generously provided. Our father is currently supplying and will continue to lavishly give from the bottomless vault of his grace. He is the only one who has sustained, is sustaining, and will sustain.

Prayer reveals the heart of need that gives way to the heart of gratitude. Prayer reminds us that He is and we are not. He is enough. He is sufficient. He is more than adequate to fulfill our inadequacy. He is home.

We have written prayers for each section of *Story Catechism* that can be prayed each time your family gathers for family worship. Every prayer is written in the context of who God is revealed to be in that piece of the catechism.

THIS IS HIS STORY...
MAY IT BE TOLD IN OUR HOMES FOR
GENERATIONS TO COME.

CREATION

GOD
EDEN
HUMANITY
TOGETHER
PERFECTION

"I had always felt life first as a story: and if there is a story there is a story-teller."
G.K. Chesterton [1]

Genesis 1v1-2
In the beginning, God created the heavens and the earth. The earth was without form and void, and darkness was over the face of the deep. And the Spirit of God was hovering over the face of the waters.

THE CREATOR GOD, THE FATHER OF ALL, CREATES. THE FULLNESS OF WHO HE IS COLLIDES WITH THE VAST EMPTINESS...

AND EVERYTHING CHANGES.

The Creator God, the Father of all, creates. The fullness of who He is collides with the vast emptiness...

And everything changes.

Light pierced the darkness... sun, moon, stars. Sky separated from land and water... Mountains, hills, prairies, and lush valleys... Oceans, lakes, rivers, and babbling streams. Trees, plants, shrubs, and flowers. Animals everywhere... Roaming, flying, slithering, and swimming.

And then, out of the divine community that has always existed, the Creator created *more*.

Man and woman, created in His image, out of His *more-ness*, invited to join him in creating. Their names were Adam and Eve.

"This is good."

"This is very good," was the Creator's refrain.

The divine invitation to join Him was an invitation to know Him and find meaning in Him. The man and woman would be with Him and learn from Him. They would participate and would be given dominion and rule over the care-taking of His creation. They would learn to co-create in the same rhythm and every expression would be a reflection of their creator. Created from more, for more, the more they would fully need would be met with complete contentment from their creator. God would perfectly provide everything they needed. The man and the woman would be without need. Everything was in its right and proper place and God would be their everything.

This storyline is the narrative of the beginnings. There was a time, when everything was good. When everything was in its right and proper place. There was deep and profound meaning, centered in the perfect love of a creator. The harmony was flawless and beautiful.

Everything was good.

CREATION catechism traces five main parts of the creation narrative in the Bible: **GOD, EDEN, HUMANITY, TOGETHER, and PERFECTION.**

01
GOD

"Our souls find satisfaction only in the God who is grand enough to worship and close enough to love. We need a home, but we also crave adventure. The greatest adventure is to seek God."
Drew Dyck [2]

In the beginning was the Word, and the Word was with God, and the Word was God. He was in the beginning with God. All things were made through him, and without him was not any thing made that was made. In him was life, and the life was the light of men. The light shines in the darkness, and the darkness has not overcome it.
John 1v1-5

God speaks, **and everything changes**.

From the opening pages in scripture, in the creation narrative, God the Creator begins to reveal who He is. Through His character and nature, He unveils the depths of His heart. In a broader sense, this is called theology. Theology defined is specifically "the study of God." It is the revelation of who God says He is, on His terms. God has revealed and is revealing Himself in and through the bible. We believe that all scripture, every word, every syllable, every dot on every i, every story reveals more and more who God says He is. The Word of God draws us to the author of the story. It woos us. It beckons us. It invites us, to the living God.

You will seek me and find me, when you seek me with all your heart.
Jeremiah 29v13

All Scripture is breathed out by God and profitable for teaching, for reproof, for correction, and for training in righteousness, that the man of God may be complete, equipped for every good work.
2 Timothy 3v16-17

At its foundation, then, theology is God revealing his character and nature. Theology is who God says He is on His terms. Brennan Manning writes that theology is "faith seeking understanding."[3] Traditionally, scholars and theologians have called these "attributes of God."

These attributes offer a glimpse into the mystery of God. The attributes of God are innumerable. The study of His character and nature is inexhaustible. It's mind-blowing to think that we can actually know God, yet it's fascinating to ponder that we can never exhaust the bottomless ocean that is God. In every nook and cranny of this world, God is exposing who He is and telling His story, from the unknown depths of the oceans to the height of Everest. From the sheer magnitude of the universe beyond us to the complexity of the universe within us. From the miracle of birth to the burden of death. Amongst fauna and flora, He is telling His story.

He is inviting us to know Him.

God is creator. He is an artist with an insanely wild imagination.
God is perfect. He alone always does what is good, right, and perfect.
God is completely and fully sufficient in and of Himself.
God is unchanging, completely consistent.
God is holy, righteous, and just.
God is powerful and present.
God is matchless in His glory.
God is good, great, and provocatively gracious.
God is patient and kind.
God is faithful. He never grows tired of putting His glory on display.
God is magnificent, full of splendor, and awe.
God is king. Out of His sovereign reign and rule, He speaks and His word is obeyed.
God is a promise maker and a promise keeper. He makes His promises and keeps His promises out of love and for His glory.
God is love. He loves with a stubborn love... *A covenant-making, commitment-keeping, grace-filled, never-leaving, without-an-exit-strategy kind of love.*

God is father. In the New Testament, the apostle Paul writes, "you have received the Spirit of adoption as sons, by whom we cry, 'Abba! Father'" (Romans 8v15). Abba literally means daddy. It is a term of tender endearment by a beloved child. As sons and daughters, with deep affection and complete dependence, we can approach God as our daddy. As a father, He provides, protects, and is perfectly present with His family. He loves with perfect precision; nothing is ever outside of our good, and everything is always for His glory. He has adopted us as His own and reminds us, "You are mine."

HE HAS ADOPTED US AS HIS OWN AND
REMINDS US, "YOU ARE MINE."

"Safe?" said Mr. Beaver; "don't you hear what Mrs. Beaver tells you? Who said anything about safe? 'Course he isn't safe. But he's good. He's the king, I tell you."

C.S. Lewis [4]

The fullness of this God collides with the vast emptiness, and He creates. He is everywhere, in all things, all the time. He was there at the beginning. He put everything in its right and proper place. He was there in pain. When death seemed to have been victorious and hope seemed lost. He was there in victory, when He triumphed over death and declared, "Oh death, where is your victory? Oh death, where is your sting?" And He will be there in the renewal and restoration of all, when He puts everything back in its right and proper place... Again!

He is God.

All of us are born with eternity set deep in our hearts, a desire for a more-ness that can only be filled by God. One of the greatest challenges we have as parents is to keep our children from settling for less.

The world offers less.

The great lie is that our heart's longing can be satisfied with the lesser things of this world. We attempt to make a god of created things instead of worshiping the creator. This is why we never find a sustained sense of satisfaction or contentment. Our hearts are longing for the more-ness of our creator. The beauty of the creation story is that it paints a picture of the one we worship. The all-powerful, all-sovereign, all-loving, all-just completeness of our God. Our struggle as parents will always be to keep the bigness of God in our homes. *As parents, we get the enormous opportunity to help our children connect the dots of their deepest desires to the source: their magnificent God.* So let's help them DREAM and let's help them to SEE the realities beyond this world. Through it all, they just might develop a taste for the kingdom of God. God is and will always be the best conversation that you can have with your children.

May our children grow up learning to dig deep wells.

READ

Genesis 1v1-2; Psalms 8v1-9, 19, 86v8-10 & v15, 90v2, 148v1-14; Hebrews 1v10, 11v3; Colossians 1v16; Revelation 4v11; Job 37v5; Isaiah 42v8; John 1v3, Isaiah 40v7-31

MEMORIZE

The beginning of the story is called: creation.
The creator is: God.
God is: perfect.
God created: everything.
God created everything: out of love and for His glory.

CHAT

Q: What did we learn about God?
A: He is the source of all that exists. He is the master artist. He creates out of love, for Himself. Psalm 90v2: everlasting to everlasting. God has always been.

Q: Who is the source of everything?
A: God. (Father, Son, Spirit)

Q: What did God create?
A: Everything. What specifically is mentioned?

Q: Why did God create?
A: For love's sake and for His glory. His love and glory are the central motives of creation.

Q: Where/how do we see the gospel?
A: Psalm 19: Creation declares God's glory. The gospel is the power of God; the psalmist writes of God's power to create new things. The gospel makes us new.

PRAY

God, You are the creator and father of everything. You are creator from the beginning of everything to the end of everything. You created out of your perfect love and for your glory alone. You alone are the source of life. Your love holds everything together. Amen.

THE BEGINNING OF THE STORY IS CALLED

CREATION.

THE CREATOR IS

GOD.

GOD IS

PERFECT.

GOD CREATED

EVERYTHING.

GOD CREATED EVERYTHING

OUT OF LOVE AND FOR HIS GLORY.

02
EDEN

Curiosity lingers in the human soul as a remnant of a time past, a reminder of a time when everything was good. We get glimpses from time to time. Feelings of déjà vu set in; "I know this feeling. I've experienced this before." These short-lived experiences quench our thirst and satisfy our souls for a fleeting blink of an eye. The pain of the human condition is pervasive and universal; eventually we awaken back to the monotony of longing. We always do.

It wasn't always this way.

In fact, it was never meant to be this way at all.

In the beginning, there was nothing but emptiness and darkness, but the creator God, in His fullness, was always there. In the nothingness, His presence hovered over the vast emptiness. The masterful artist had a stunning plan. Like a painter starting with a blank canvas, the creator God began to create. From His fullness, He created in the empty space. But instead of using paint and brushes, He spoke. God displayed His complete and total sovereign authority over everything by simply using His voice.

*The **voice** of the LORD is over the waters; the God of glory thunders, the LORD, over many waters. The **voice** of the LORD is powerful; the **voice** of the LORD is full of majesty. The **voice** of the LORD breaks the cedars; the LORD breaks the cedars of Lebanon. He makes Lebanon to skip like a calf, and Sirion like a young wild ox. The **voice** of the LORD flashes forth flames of fire. The **voice** of the LORD shakes the wilderness; the LORD shakes the wilderness of Kadesh. The **voice** of the LORD makes the deer give birth and strips the forests bare, and in his temple all cry, "Glory!"*
Psalm 29v3-9

Nothingness began to take shape. He spoke and everything changed. Light pierced the darkness, and creation took on new life. The love story of Eden comes into being.

"And God saw that it was good."

The creation narrative in the bible tells of a place called Eden. A story filled with wonder and awe, romance and splendor; exploration and discovery in every breath. With each new step, deep and profound meaning was topped with unadulterated bliss. There was pure freedom and wide-eyed wonder, a world filled with complete and total harmony. God and His creation were entwined as a symphony, matched with resonance and consonance. All of creation was singing the same song, in tune with the heart of its creator. Birds chirping, the babbling of lazy streams, the rustling of leaves; the new creation was singing. Everything was in its right and proper place. Everything was created perfectly to sustain life and the vibrant experiences of ecstasy.

The bible says Eden was beautiful, with a garden. And it was perfect. "And the LORD God planted a garden in Eden, in the east..." (Genesis 2v8). One river diverged into four separate rivers that fed the land and made it fertile and optimal for life. Eden was special. Eden was spectacular. But make no mistake: that which was special about Eden was God Himself. His presence presided over Eden. Everything He created reflected who He was and what He was like. The Bible says that God walked in the garden in the cool of the day. He was there, His spirit everywhere, His fingerprints on everything.

Eden was home because the creator, the father God, was there.

Eden was home because God is home.

"Our heart is made to live in a larger story; having lost that we do the best we can by developing our own smaller dramas."
Brent Curtis & John Eldredge [6]

Armed with fabricated fairytales and computer-generated mythical worlds, most times it's difficult to imagine Eden being an actual place. And if it's difficult to imagine Eden as real, then it increasingly becomes more difficult to connect with a story like we have in the creation narrative. We don't live in Eden. We live in a world full of dissonance and discord, exploitation and agenda. Out of tune, the melody out of whack, off pitch, our world sings the song of brokenness. We are constantly confronted with and presented as damaged goods. The pictures and imagery we get from Eden are difficult to relate with. We know nothing of the garden life here and now, yet Eden whispers.

Where is Eden now?

If Eden has more to do with God than it does the garden life, perhaps when we wonder, "Where is Eden now?" we are really asking, "Where is God in all of this?" In all of the suffering, in all of the pain, in all of the questions, in all of the confusion.

God, have you forgotten about us?

But Eden echoes...

He is here.
He is present.
He is with us.
There is more, still.

In Eden, we find the heart of God on full display. From his perfection and goodness, He designed all that is perfect and good. It's hard for us to understand the beauty of Eden because we've never experienced true Eden. But we can imagine the beauty when we recognize the things we do not find in Eden, the very things we spend most of our lives trying to escape. Grueling work, difficult relationships, failed parenting, strained friendships, even the shame of the lack of personal holiness. Life feels as if there is always a constant current of opposition flowing against us, doesn't it? Sin taints everything and makes all of life so much more difficult. It becomes hard to find joy at work. It's difficult to sustain oneness with our spouse. We constantly feel like we are looking failure in the eye. As parents, friends, brothers and sisters, sons and daughters, husbands and wives, and disciples of Christ, failure seems to lurk around every corner. "Not good enough" follows closely behind. Eden reminds us that God's design is not congruent with common experience. God is good, and His plan of redemption is bringing us back to a place of His goodness. If we do not keep Eden in mind, we might think that this present struggle represents God more than the goodness of Eden would. If we do not keep Eden in mind, our hearts can become numb or bitter and we stop looking to God for refuge and relief and stop hoping in God for our rescue. We will find short-lived refuge in temporary things instead of an abiding home in God. Our invitation as parents is to help our children, to guide them to the heart of the Father and the great hope in His love. Our call is to journey with them, to show them so they can see and know God's heart for them. We are to pilgrimage in His goodness, set our feet in His perfection, and experience belonging. Eden is our first picture of the goodness of God, and it is that very goodness on which we need to learn to rely every day.

This is home.

He is home.

May our children grow to know and experience the goodness of God.

READ

Genesis 1v3-25, 1v31, 2v4-25; Jeremiah 17v7-8; Psalm 17v1, 27v1, 46v9-5

MEMORIZE

At the beginning of the story there is a: garden.
The garden is called: Eden.
Eden was a place where everything was in its: right and proper place.
And God said: it is good.
It was good because: God is good and He was there.

CHAT

Q: What did we learn about God?
A: God makes beautiful things. God is the one who puts everything in its right place. Eden was created out of love and for God. True, real love made Eden special.

Q: What do you think it means that everything was in its right and proper place?
A: God is good, right, and perfect, so all He does is good, right, and perfect.

Q: What do you think God meant when he said "it is very good"?
A: There was no mistake. God created out of love and fullness. Creation was perfect. Everything was separated perfectly into its specific place and category.

Q: What did Eden represent?
A: Goodness, love, rightness, home, belonging, relationship, worship. Eden represented God.

Q: Where/how do we see the gospel?
A: We see God's power on display. There is now life where there was once nothing.

PRAY

God, everything that is good is from You and for You. In You, all things are held together perfectly. Every stitch is placed perfectly for Your glory. In You, everything finds its meaning and purpose. Like an anchor, Your love holds everything together.

AT THE BEGINNING OF THE STORY THERE IS A

GARDEN.

THE GARDEN IS CALLED

EDEN.

EDEN WAS A PLACE WHERE EVERYTHING WAS IN ITS

RIGHT AND PROPER PLACE.

AND GOD SAID

IT IS GOOD.

IT WAS GOOD BECUASE

GOD IS GOOD AND HE WAS THERE.

03
HUMANITY

The echoes of Eden reverberate off the walls of the hearts of humanity. The desire for more is always within us. It seems the human experience is one of an insatiable desire to satisfy our deep hunger, to quench the deep thirst of our soul. Our longings only show the depth of who we are and who we were created to be.

Where does the longing for more come from?

Why does the desire for more feel primal and natural?

Then God said, "Let us make man in our image, after our likeness. And let them have dominion over the fish of the sea and over the birds of the heavens and over the livestock and over all the earth and over every creeping thing that creeps on the earth." So God created man in his own image, in the image of God he created him; male and female he created them.
Genesis 1v26-27

God looked over His creation and saw that it was good. With each new addition, like a master architect, He purposefully placed with perfect precision everything that was necessary for sustained perfection. Being fully present, and with His spirit presiding over all of creation, He saw that *it was good*.

Then, He created more.

There is a deep and profound shift in the twenty-sixth and twenty-seventh verses of the first chapter of Genesis. The narrative seems to place more intention and purpose on this moment with the subtle shift in language. The writer uses communal language when referring to God in the moment of creating humanity. God said, "Let **us** make man in **our** image, after **our** likeness." Out of his "us-ness" and "our-ness" God forms man. From this divine community of God the Father, God the Son, and God the Spirit, humanity is created. Created from the likeness of this divine community, humanity bears the image of God. Described by the Latin phrase imago dei, which means image of God, humanity differs from everything else in the creation narrative. You and I, your neighbor and your coworker, the homeless beggar and the doctor, the light-skinned and the dark-skinned, male and female; we all bear the blueprint of our maker. The more-ness of God; the imago dei, is within every human being. Perhaps the natural inclination and insatiable desire for more comes directly from our primal design. We crave more because we were created from more and for more. Just as the fingerprints of the creator were over everything in Eden, the breath of God is in every human being.

...then the LORD God formed the man of dust from the ground and breathed into his nostrils the breath of life, and the man became a living creature.
Genesis 2v7

In the creation narrative, we read that God took the dust of the ground, formed it, shaped it, and then breathed into it. The scriptures say God breathed the breath of life into the man. The divine collides with the dust, and life bursts forth. Interestingly, one of the English translations for both the Old Testament Hebrew word and the New Testament Greek word for *breath* is the word *spirit*. When God breathed His breath into the dust, He breathed His Spirit into the lifeless pile of dirt. The very spirit of God was breathed into humanity. With His lungs full of the breath of the living God, Adam opened his eyes and met his creator.

With each inhale
        he breathes deeply anew the breath of God,
                and with every exhale
                        the creator receives back his breath.

The new cadence of inhale and exhale joins the worshipful refrain in the song of creation.

Created with deep meaning and purpose, humanity enters the story.

All of creation worships.

And God said, "It was very good."

From the beginning, God says, "You are mine." Like a groom who stands confidently beckoning his bride as she prepares to walk towards him, receiving the invitation; from this day forward, "You are mine." By divine decree and created order, humanity was and is the apex of His creation. The crowning jewel in the crown of creation. Created to reflect Him, to be with Him, work with Him, and join Him. God created this vibrantly perfect world, then He placed humanity in it and provided perfectly everything humanity needed. A perfect world, fit for sustained perfection. Beauty gave birth to more beauty. Eden was home; God was there. Adam and Eve found deep meaning and profound purpose in their creator. God would be their everything.

Everything was good.
    Everything was right.
        God would never stop loving His children.

I (David) send my 11-year-old daughter off to school almost every morning. I kiss her on the head and I say, "*Remember who made you.*" She's at that age where it's becoming embarrassing for her, especially if her friends are walking by. It's simple, I get it; it's a tad bit cheesy, I know, but I keep doing it because I can hear the whisper of the world in my subconscious mind. I see the billboards and ads telling a different story. The flood of whispers, the deluge of images, the onslaught of advertisements, all converging, all trying to convince my daughter that *beautiful* is nothing more than a waist size or a bust size that seeks attention. "*Remember who made you,*" I whisper back. As a father, the whispers of the world terrify me. What is even worse is that I know at the core of my heart that no matter how much I tell her it's not true (I do as often as I get the opportunity), the only way she will believe it is if she knows the beauty of the one who made her. "*Remember who made you.*" I'll forever remind her, until she believes that her creator is the one who paints the sunsets and hangs the stars, that He forms mountains and chooses the colors of her favorite flowers, that He was the one who formed her in her mother's womb. Until she knows this truth, she will allow some other person or idea to define beauty for her.

What makes creation beautiful is not its beholder, but its creator.

The world tries hard to put a value on life, and in the process it has destroyed much of God's beautiful creation. Whether physically or emotionally, through genocide, abortion, or the exploitation of women, when the world tries to set life's value, life becomes a product that is used for consumption. We, however, were not created for that purpose, but rather to reflect the image of the one who created us. When we imagine the magnificence of all of the created things in the beginning and then realize that the master artist had not yet created His most magnificent work until He created us, it is only then that we change the way we see ourselves and one another.

Remember who made you.

Remember who you are.

May our children grow to know the source that defines beauty and gives life.

READ

Genesis 1v26-27; Genesis 2v4-7; Genesis 2v18-23; Psalm 139v14; Ephesians 1v4-6; Genesis 5v1-2; Psalm 8v3-8; 2 Corinthians 5v17-20

MEMORIZE

God's most special creation was: man and woman.
Their names were: Adam and Eve.
They were special because: they were created in God's image.
To be created in God's image means: to represent Him and glorify Him.
And then God said: it is very good.

CHAT

Q: Why were man and woman most special or different from the rest of creation?
A: They were created in God's image. Chat about how our sons and daughters have bits and pieces of us in them: personalities, physical features, behavior, etc.

Q: How do we represent God every day?
A: Everything was created out of love. God creates us to join Him and be with Him, to show the world His love.

Q: What does it mean to be created in the image of God?
A: God is more. God created us out of his "moreness." When we desire more, we desire Him.

Q: What did we learn about God?
A: God clearly does not need us. He puts His glory on display through us to show His glory.

Q: Where/how do we see the gospel?
A: The image of God will be clearly seen in Jesus, God the Son.

PRAY

God, everything You create is a masterpiece, but Your crowning stroke and most beautiful showpiece is me. Flesh and blood, skin and bones, fingers and toes... a soul with a body created for the world to know You and experience Your love. Your love holds everything together. Amen.

GOD'S MOST SPECIAL CREATION WAS
MAN AND WOMAN.
THEIR NAMES WERE
ADAM AND EVE.
THEY WERE SPECIAL BECAUSE
THEY WERE CREATED IN GOD'S IMAGE.
TO BE CREATED IN GOD'S IMAGE MEANS
TO REPRESENT HIM AND GLORIFY HIM.
AND THEN GOD SAID
IT IS VERY GOOD.

04
TOGETHER

Every faculty you have, your power of thinking or of moving your limbs from moment to moment, is given you by God. If you devoted every moment of your whole life exclusively to His service, you could not give Him anything that was not in a sense His own already.
C. S. Lewis [7]

The existence of humanity is not the result of some random cosmic force. The creator God, with deep intention and profound purpose, knew exactly what He intended to do and whom He was creating. There was something special about man and woman, something unique. Humanity was unlike the rest of creation, and it would reflect the heart of its creator unlike anything else in His world. Full of purpose and intention, he designed humans for a specific invitation. After the design was complete, God saw fit to bless them. After bestowing them with uniqueness and blessing them, in one momentous transference of responsibility and authority, the creator invited His creation to join Him in creating.

And God blessed them. And God said to them, "Be fruitful and multiply and fill the earth and subdue it, and have dominion over the fish of the sea and over the birds of the heavens and over every living thing that moves on the earth."
Genesis 1v28

As co-creators and co-conspirators, the man and the woman received instructions to steward God's creation and to cultivate this new relationship. "Be with me and take care of my creation" was the heart of the creator. This new call to stewardship was not just a call to maintain His creation, but an invitation to participate; it was an invitation to multiply and create with Him. The call to steward and cultivate was about the Father's glory. Through no means of their own and with no way to earn the invitation, the man and the woman received the gift of participation. Fashioned with deep meaning, gifted with great purpose, the man and the woman join the creator God in his work.

The earth is the LORD's, and everything in it, the world, and all who live in it.
Psalm 24v1

This is the foundational principle in understanding stewardship: everything belongs to God. In humanity's original design and intent, God creates co-creators to be with Him and join Him in creating. Thus, the ability to work is a gift and a sacred practice. Work is an opportunity to worship, as we join God in the everyday invitation to represent Him. However menial or mundane the task, the ability to work is a gift. The responsibility then, is to steward the gift. To steward is to administer or manage on behalf of someone else. The creator God gives Adam and Eve a sense of ownership, a call to partner, a piece of dominion. The man and the woman are to cultivate the relationship between themselves and his creation, all as a response of their relationship and union with Him. "Everything you see is mine! As my ambassadors and co-creators, take care of my creation and enjoy all of it."

The original intent to bless in order to give the blessing away still rings true today. Created for more, invited to participate with God on His mission, we experience His constant pursuit and consistent provision. Steward your blessing; take responsibility for the unique gift given to you. "Show the world who I am and what I look like. Represent and reveal. Join me." We find something destructive happens to the human soul when the blessing ends with us. We were never created to hoard our blessings. Our hearts weren't built that way. From the beginning of the story, we discover that creator God was pleased and satisfied with His creation. His refrain? "It is good." But this chorus changed a bit after Adam. Created from the likeness and the fullness of God, Adam was given invitation and authority. Adam was to cultivate and contribute to creation. He would take part in care taking and overseeing. And God saw that it was no longer just good, it was "very good."

This is the bedrock of God as promise maker. Nothing has changed. We know innately, deep within our being, that we were created for more. This narrative was placed at the center of our makeup. "*I gave you your identity. I gave you your name. I created you and made you free. You are mine. Now, be with me. Join me. Work with me.*"

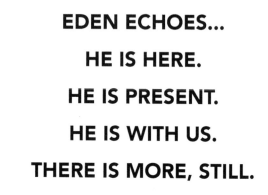

EDEN ECHOES...
HE IS HERE.
HE IS PRESENT.
HE IS WITH US.
THERE IS MORE, STILL.

So often, we are convinced that the "more" our hearts long for is a tangible thing. Maybe an accomplishment or accolade, perhaps a relationship or an experience. The problem we experience with all of those *things* is that they are temporary. They fade away with every passing minute, like dandelions in late spring. What our children need is not another carrot dangled in front of them promising happiness and delight. What our family needs is much more primal and much deeper. We long to know who we are and why we were made. Is this not the most pondered and pontificated question in the universe? The question that has launched endless pilgrimages and pursuits in search of transcendence? Pilgrims and poets, kings and peasants alike, searching endlessly on the quest for meaning and purpose. It is in the purposes of God that our hearts will find satisfaction and rest. It is in participation with the Father that we begin to understand the wholeness that comes from walking within God's design. Learning to help our children ask the right questions will be one of the most formative things we can learn as parents. We cultivate the environments of our homes, like master gardeners, prepping the ground of their hearts and tilling the fertile soil to be receptive to gospel seeds. Learning to ask more *why* alongside of *what* will allow for more conversation to naturally emerge. "Why do you want to do it?" in addition to "what do you want to do?" gives us a window into the hearts of our children. I (Freddy) pray my boys know there is no question off-limits. I pray that our connection as father and son(s) will push the boundaries further out and light will shine brightly, allowing us to address areas of hidden shame and regret. We are a people who were designed to live *from* our identity, not *for* it. Whether a doctor, plumber, or teacher, we teach our children the sacredness in all of our activities comes from whether or not we are participating with the Father. We tend to participate either for Him or apart from Him, but our satisfaction will only come when we participate *with* Him.

May we invite our families to find rhythm in participating with God in His rhythms.

READ

Genesis 1v28-31, 2v15; 1 Chronicles 29v11-12; Job 42v2

MEMORIZE

It was God's desire that man and woman would always: be with Him and take care of His creation.
God would always: love Adam and Eve and take care of them.
Because God was faithful, God would always: provide everything they needed.
Eden was home because: God was with them.
God was in control and had: complete authority.

CHAT

Q: What do we need? What do we need the most?
A: Water, food, money, shelter, clothes, relationships, etc... but we need Jesus more than anything, he provides grace.

Q: How does God faithfully provide what we need?
A: Jobs to work hard and earn money; then we must learn how to spend our money.

Q: What did God trust humanity with? How can we/do we take care of God's creation?
A: To take care of creation.

Q: What did we learn about God?
A: Like a good father, God wants to be with us, take care of us, faithfully provide for us, and sustain us. He has complete authority.

Q: Where/how do we see the gospel?
A: God provides perfectly. He knew Jesus was the only way to give us all we need.

PRAY

God, thank you. You created us to always and forever be with You. You promise to always take care of us and invite us to join You in taking care of Your creation and everything in it. You alone are always faithful in every way. You are everything we need. Your love holds everything together. Amen.

IT WAS GOD'S DESIRE THAT MAN AND WOMAN WOULD ALWAYS

BE WITH HIM

AND TAKE CARE OF HIS CREATION.

GOD WOULD ALWAYS

LOVE ADAM AND EVE
AND TAKE CARE OF THEM.

BECAUSE GOD WAS FAITHFUL, GOD WOULD ALWAYS

PROVIDE EVERYTHING
THEY NEEDED.

EDEN WAS HOME BECAUSE

GOD WAS WITH THEM.

GOD WAS IN CONTROL AND HAD

COMPLETE AUTHORITY.

05
PERFECTION

"*A child kicks his legs rhythmically through excess, not an absence of life. Because children have abounding vitality, because they are in spirit fierce and free, therefore they want things repeated and unchanged. They always say, "Do it again"; and the grown-up person does it again until he is nearly dead. For grown-up people are not strong enough to exult in monotony. But perhaps God is strong enough to exult in monotony. It is possible that God says every morning, "Do it again" to the sun; and every evening, "Do it again" to the moon. It may not be automatic necessity that makes all daisies alike; it may be that God makes every daisy separately, but has never got tired of making them.*"
Zach Eswine [8]

O God, you are my God; earnestly I seek you; my soul thirsts for you; my flesh faints for you, as in a dry and weary land where there is no water. So I have looked upon you in the sanctuary, beholding your power and glory. Because your steadfast love is better than life, my lips will praise you. So I will bless you as long as I live; in your name I will lift up my hands. My soul will be satisfied as with fat and rich food, and my mouth will praise you with joyful lips, when I remember you upon my bed, and meditate on you in the watches of the night; for you have been my help, and in the shadow of your wings I will sing for joy." My soul clings to you; your right hand upholds me.
Psalm 63v1-8

We are image-bearers of the divine community, created from the blueprint of the very character and nature of God, invited to participate, represent, and reveal. This is *who* we are. This is *what* we were created to do. This is *how* we were created to live.

Eden was whole.

Eden was complete.

Eden was perfect.

With everything in its right and proper place, creation found its identity in relation to the creator. The idea of wholeness and completeness is close to heart of the Jewish people in the Old Testament. The Hebrews knew this concept by the word *shalom*, the Hebrew word for peace. More than just the absence of conflict, it encompasses the idea of wholeness and completeness. Eden was physical and tangible shalom. A technicolor, three-dimensional, high-definition picture of freedom. It looked like, smelled like, tasted like, felt like, sounded like the heart of its creator. The psalmist writes, "Oh, taste and see that the Lord is good" (Psalm 34v8). Eden was chockfull of shalom, beckoning creation to indulge in its shelter. Adam and Eve experienced the full shalom of God. Everything had an overall sense of wholeness and replicated the complete sufficiency of the creator. Eden was fashioned in deep meaning and purpose.

Humanity never stopped longing for *shalom*.

There is a garden-longing within the human soul.

At the center of humanity exists a constant longing. An unquenchable thirst and desire for more. Rarely satisfied with what this world has to offer us, we set out in daily search for transcendence. We are innately drawn to words like "beyond," "horizon," and "adventure." We experience a constant push to explore, imagine, dream, and learn.

Is it possible that every one of these lingering moments is meant to arouse our curiosity?

Is it possible that in the midst of monotony, we are created to collide into these lingering moments; to remind us there is more?

Is it possible that these lingering moments are an oasis in a desert? A grace-filled moment to remember that God never grows tired of his faithfulness.

Space to breathe.

Moments to feel.

Opportunities to remember.

There is a great paradox at the heart of humanity. We are full of profound purpose and intention, yet we are fragile, created from dust. The Hebrew word for ground is *adamah*. From *adamah* we get *Adam*. Formed from the ground, Adam's name represents his origins.

Created from the dust of the ground, the origins of humanity are of fragile beginnings. The writer of Ecclesiastes says, "All go to one place. All are from the dust, and to dust all return" (Ecclesiastes 3v20). The psalmist writes, "For he knows our frame; he remembers that we are dust" (Psalm 103v14). We are fragile, needy, and vulnerable, made from dust. Yet paradoxically, we possess the breath of life. Created in the image of God, brought to life through His spirit, the more-ness of God is at the center of the architecture of humanity. The breath of the sovereign, masterful creator was given to us.

Though fragile, we were made for more.

The apostle Paul, in the New Testament, in the letter written to the church in Corinth borrows this imagery. He writes, "But we have this treasure in jars of clay, to show that the surpassing power belongs to God and not to us" (2 Corinthians 4v7). Clay was an everyday, common, and cheap material, yet God saw it fit to place treasure in these jars. We are the jars of clay; the everyday, normal, ordinary, common, and fragile material. His spirit dwells in us, and the fullness of Jesus reveals his authority, power and greatness in the lives of humanity.

"The glory of God is man fully alive."
St. Iraneas [9]

We are most alive when God's glory is on display in our lives. When the moments of more collide with the often-tread terrain of numb and dull, we remember. This may be the origin of such phrases as "*breathtaking*" and "*my heart skipped a beat.*" What if Niagara Falls, Yosemite, the Grand Canyon, the majestic pines of the Rockies, were all created to remind us? A kiss, a smell, a taste, all to connect our longing to something more? When tragedy strikes and suffering sneaks up on us; when we're left wondering, questioning, and doubting, all this for what? These undeserved moments of grace and surprise woo us back. The invitation to join in the symphony of creation and participate in the rhythm of the creator reminds us.

There is more.

You were created for more,

Herein lies the great tension of the human experience. In our best attempts and on our best days, we are constantly reminded of our frailness while simultaneously aware of our more-ness. We get tired. We get exhausted. We find ourselves emotionally and physically at the "end of our ropes." We swing back and forth; we ebb and flow; we rise and fall. We are perpetually unfaithful. We are frail, weak, and fragile. We often find ourselves in places and moments of hopelessness. We have tried and failed innumerable times. We've been let down, burned, and neglected in countless ways. The difficult monotony of the human condition leaves us weary. The everyday, monotonous grind of the depravity of the human experience leaves us empty, exhausted, wear, and desperate.

Most days we feel too broken to fly, unable to hide the growing cracks of unbelief.

Our desperation increases.

But the father of all, the creator God never grows weary. He never tires of His great faithfulness. He never gets fatigued from putting His glory on display. He is endlessly, tirelessly, and perpetually faithful. He alone always does what is good, right, and perfect. He doesn't swing back and forth like a pendulum in seismic shifts. He doesn't ebb and flow with the tides of culture. He doesn't rise and fall with the kingdoms of our age.

He is faithful.

He is more.

He now chooses to put His glory on display through his church: you, me, us... the broken, frail, fragile ones, the perpetually unfaithful ones, the people who incessantly run to lovers less wild...

Why me? Aren't the Rockies more spectacular than me? Yosemite more grand than I? This is still one of the greatest questions and mysteries to grapple. The apostle Paul writes that God invites us to represent Him. Paul even calls us ambassadors and says that God is making His appeal through us (*2 Corinthians 5v20*). The father and creator of all, the one who never tires of putting his glory on display, is revealing to the world who He is through His active work in us, His church. The words of St. Iraneas echo in our hearts: "The glory of God is man fully alive," as if He were making His appeal through us. God the Father shows himself perfectly through His son Jesus. Through Jesus's life, death, and resurrection, He reconciles us back to His father and now sends the church to show what He is like and how He loves. He is making his appeal through you... me... us... His church.

He is still creating.

He is bringing *shalom* again.

Have you considered this question lately? How has God put His glory on display through your life? Today? This week? This month?

How are you experiencing the daily movement of the gospel in your life?

I know for me, (Freddy) more often than not, I find myself in the monotonous grind of what feels like assembly line production. In season and out, each new day, more the same, I miss the subtle beauty that passes by without notice, without even a glance. But what if we became *noticers*? Intentional awareness--eyes fully open, hearts awake and ready with perpetual and endless fascination of what today has to offer. What may seem like inconsequential details to most; smells, tones, colors, ambient noises in the background, random passersby, become the setting, cast, and soundtrack for the moment. The monotony takes on new life. The mundane receives a new heartbeat. My youngest son is insatiably curious. Like most six-year-olds, he still approaches most things with wide-eyed wonder. By night's end, he's easily logged hundreds of questions, many of which have gone unanswered or simply ignored. Admittedly, sometimes the questions wear me out and I tell him he has only has three more questions for the evening. I need to remind him to use them wisely, because inevitably the first question has something to do with why can he only ask three more questions before bed?

All behavior is rooted in belief.

My youngest son repeats this approach to life day after day after day. This behavior is rooted in a deep belief that there is more. His curiosity compels him to notice. His fascination pushes him further into awareness. He believes there is more, so he lives as if there is more. He believes I know more than he does, so he thinks I can answer every question he asks. Truth is, all our behavior is rooted in belief. The garden of everyday life blooms from the soil of belief and unbelief. Every act reveals a deeper piece of who we are and who we believe God to be. This truth invites us to wrestle with belief more than just seek to modify our children's behaviors. This invitation welcomes questions and beckons exploration over indoctrination. If life is ultimately about behavior more than belief, our lives will tend to vacillate between wins and losses. We will find pride in our victories and shame in our defeats—elevated pride when "all is well" and thwarted pride when things didn't turn out "the way they were supposed to be." All of life will be one great performance. We will be defined as champions of our last achievement or victims of our latest blow. Performance addicts eventually become approval addicts and people pleasers. Our children will grow up looking to please us rather than love us. But there is a bigger vision and grand invitation.

Life is more than karaoke.
It's more than charades.

There is something more, something deeper.

Freedom beckons.
  Freedom calls.
    Freedom invites.

May our children grow up beyond the comparisons, beyond anxious performance, and beyond the restlessness of joyless duty.

READ

Genesis 2v16-17 & v25; Galatians 5v1; Psalm 119v1-8; 1 John 4

MEMORIZE

They trusted God and: believed in Him.
Adam and Eve loved God so they: obeyed Him.
In love and obedience: there is always freedom.
Eden was: perfect and complete.
God was their: everything.

CHAT

Q: Whom do you trust the most? Why?
A: They love us, they know what is right, they keep us safe. We innately know to trust love (connect dots to the beginnings), because we were created out of love.

Q: Why did Adam and Eve trust and obey God?
A: God loved them and took care of them. He was good and faithful to them.

Q: What is obedience? What is freedom?
A: Obedience is an act of love. Where there is trust, belief, love, and obedience, there is freedom. I know I AM LOVED.

Q: What did we learn about God?
A: He is trustworthy. This question is always before us: is God trustworthy?

Q: Where/how do we see the gospel?
A: There is only freedom in love. The cross is the single greatest act of love and obedience.

PRAY

God, You are faithful. Help us in our unbelief. God, You are good and full of grace. We don't have to look elsewhere to find what we are looking for. You are all-satisfying, and in You, there is nothing left to do. Like a bird that flies free, may our hearts know Your boundless love. Your love holds everything together. Amen.

THEY TRUSTED GOD AND **BELIEVED IN HIM.** ADAM AND EVE LOVED GOD SO THEY **OBEYED HIM.** IN LOVE AND OBEDIENCE **THERE IS ALWAYS FREEDOM.** EDEN WAS **PERFECT AND COMPLETE.** GOD WAS THEIR **EVERYTHING.**

REBELLION

THE ADVERSARY
THE GREAT LIE
THE SHAME
THE CONSEQUENCE
THE DESPERATION

Isaiah 14v12-15
How you have fallen from heaven, morning star, son of the dawn! You have been cast down to the earth, you who once laid low the nations! You said in your heart, "I will ascend to the heavens; I will raise my throne above the stars of God; I will ascend above the tops of the clouds; I will make myself like the Most High." But you are brought down to the realm of the dead, to the depths of the pit.

WE WERE DESIGNED WITH AN
INSATIABLE AND RELENTLESS DESIRE
FOR LOVE. WE ARE DESIGNED FOR GOD.
OUR DESIRE FOR GOD IS FIERCE. GOD'S
LOVE FOR HIS BELOVED IS FEROCIOUS.

We are image bearers of the divine community. Created from the blueprint of the very character and nature of God, invited to join and participate, to represent and reveal. Created unique and with deep purpose, humanity was the crowning jewel of creation. Created from the likeness of the divine community, the desire for more was placed at the heart of Adam and Eve. The master artist created a beautiful world and placed them in it. Given authority and invited to join the creator God as co-creators, the man and woman would be responsible to cultivate and oversee God's creation. God provided perfectly everything they needed. They loved God and trusted Him. They believed God and obeyed Him. God was their everything!

This is *who* we are. This is *what* we were created to do. This is *how* we were created to live.

Eden was whole.

Eden was complete.

Eden was perfect.

As co-creators and stewards of God's creation, they were free to indulge. God had created everything for them, and as any good father would, he loved to see them enjoy His creation. But their newly-given freedom came with responsibility. The invitation to take care of His creation came with a promise. The man and the woman were free to delight in everything and anything, including eating any fruit from any tree in the entire garden, except the fruit of one specific tree. He called it the tree of the knowledge of good and evil.

And the LORD God commanded the man, saying, "You may surely eat of every tree of the garden, but of the tree of the knowledge of good and evil you shall not eat, for in the day that you eat of it you shall surely die."
Genesis 2v16-17

The fruit of that tree would become the battleground of their hearts. The man and woman would be deceived into doubting God. What seemed like a simple, no-big-deal, no-one-will-ever-know kind of act would painfully and tragically change everything. It would be a rebellious act of treason.

Our rebellion, which is to say our sin, severed the perfect relationship humanity was created to have with our creator God. The tactic? Deception. The distortion of truth was that man and woman didn't need God anymore, that they would be okay without Him, and that they could find their own way.

Things are no longer as they should be. What was once our source of pleasure, enjoyment, contentment, and satisfaction would become the soul's deepest chasm. Since that tragic moment of rebellion in the garden of Eden, found in the opening pages of scripture in the creation narrative, humanity has been in a constant pursuit of discovery and connection, trying once again to know its identity... trying to find its story. We believe our identity is found in the roots of God's love story, the Gospel.

REBELLION catechism traces five main parts of the deception and the distortion of truth: **THE ADVERSARY, THE GREAT LIE, THE SHAME, THE CONSEQUENCE, and THE DESPERATION.**

06
THE ADVERSARY

"How you are fallen from heaven, O Day Star, son of Dawn! How you are cut down to the ground, you who laid the nations low! You said in your heart, 'I will ascend to heaven; above the stars of God I will set my throne on high; I will sit on the mount of assembly in the far reaches of the north; I will ascend above the heights of the clouds; I will make myself like the Most High.' But you are brought down to Sheol, to the far reaches of the pit."
Isaiah 14v12-15

In all great stories, there is always an enemy, a villain, known as the narrative's antagonist. The adversary attempts to thwart and oppose someone or something, most often the hero of the story, at all costs. This enemy is hostile to the ways of the hero. His one purpose is the destruction of all that the hero loves. The adversary, in the story seeks to strike God's heart via what He loves most dearly: us, His beloved.

The enemy in the biblical narrative is called many names; Satan, the adversary, the devil, the dragon, Lucifer, Beelzebub, the ruler of darkness, the tempter, and the thief, among many others. The apostle Peter writes, "Your adversary, the devil, prowls around like a roaring lion, seeking someone to devour" (1 Peter 5v8). John writes that "the thief comes only to steal, kill, and destroy" (John 10v10).

The hostile adversary, full of hate and deception, shows up early in the creation narrative in Eden. In Genesis chapter three, he takes on the form of a serpent. But this isn't where Satan's story begins. In the Old Testament, we find passages that refer to evil kings. These passages give very clear and distinct narratives that describe the evil one who is behind the actions of these evil kings. The Bible says that Satan was one of God's most powerful and beautiful created beings, specifically an angelic being called a cherub. In their heavenly state, a cherub was a large and towering creature. According to Ezekiel's vision, all cherubim (plural for cherub) were eighteen feet tall and had four wings reaching a span of eight feet. Under their wings were hands like humans. Each being had four faces, as well. One face was that of a cherub, one face was that of a man, one face a lion, and the last an eagle. Their entire bodies were covered in eyes (Ez. 10). The book of Revelation similarly describes these beings with faces of a lion, an ox, a man, and an eagle. Each had sets of six wings. Day and night they never stopped worshipping, reciting over and over again, "Holy, holy, holy is the Lord God Almighty, who was and is and is to come" (Revelation 4v6-8). The cherubim symbolize God's holy, set-apart presence, and His unapproachable, grand majesty. These angelic creatures are given specific and unique roles in scripture. They were created to guard and protect the holiness of God.

In Isaiah, Satan is called Lucifer, which, translated from the original Hebrew word, means *brightness*. Often referred to as the "bright and morning star," he is even described as the "anointed cherub" (Ez. 28v14). He was the highest creature God had ever created. "You were the seal of perfection, full of wisdom and perfect in beauty" (Ez. 28v12). Satan was given the highest, most exalted position in all of creation...

But he wanted more.

> *"You were the signet of perfection, full of wisdom and perfect in beauty. You were in Eden, the garden of God; every precious stone was your covering, sardius, topaz, and diamond, beryl, onyx, and jasper, sapphire, emerald, and carbuncle; and crafted in gold were your settings and your engravings. On the day that you were created they were prepared. You were an anointed guardian cherub. I placed you; you were on the holy mountain of God; in the midst of the stones of fire you walked. You were blameless in your ways from the day you were created, till unrighteousness was found in you. In the abundance of your trade you were filled with violence in your midst, and you sinned; so I cast you as a profane thing from the mountain of God, and I destroyed you, O guardian cherub, from the midst of the stones of fire. Your heart was proud because of your beauty; you corrupted your wisdom for the sake of your splendor. I cast you to the ground; I exposed you before kings, to feast their eyes on you.*
> **Ezekiel 28v12-17**

Satan wasn't content with the position and privilege of honor bestowed upon him. His perfection and beauty turned into pride and he wanted the highest, most glorious of all positions. He wanted to be God. Isaiah writes that he said, "*I will ascend to heaven; above the stars of God I will set my throne on high; I will sit on the mount of assembly in the far reaches of the north; I will ascend above the heights of the clouds; I will make myself like the Most High.*" Discontented with being God's servant, he sought to become the one who would be served. Convincing a third of the angels to join his rebellion, he mounted an attack against God and set his sight on the throne.

Now war arose in heaven, Michael and his angels fighting against the dragon. And the dragon and his angels fought back, but he was defeated, and there was no longer any place for them in heaven. And the great dragon was thrown down, that ancient serpent, who is called the devil and Satan, the deceiver of the whole world—he was thrown down to the earth, and his angels were thrown down with him.
Revelation 12v7-9

God's army, led by the archangel Michael, defeated Satan and his insurrection. Satan's attempt to overthrow God was overcome. God, in his holiness, righteousness, and perfection, does not allow sin to remain in His presence. So in his defeat, Satan was forced from his position in the heavenly realm, to the lower parts, earth, where he continues to wage war and rebellion against God's creation. The adversary goes to extreme lengths to weave his tapestry of lies and deception. He is cunning and he is ruthless, seeking to devour and destroy all that is good. In defeat, he now aims his tactic at the heart of humanity. Still desiring to be worshipped, he attempts to woo humanity into the ways of rebellion.

In the midst of disciplining our children, discipleship can be difficult. Disobedience is painful. The older our children become, the more painfully and acutely we feel the rejection. The harsher their words become, the louder their voices raise, the more readily we try to fix and control. Emotions run high, frustration ever-present before us. It seems easier to flex our authority in an attempt to fix behavior than to humbly pursue our children's hearts. Feeling rejected and dishonored, we set out to regain our rightful position.

A few years ago, when my (Freddy) youngest son was about five years old, my wife caught him in a moment of deliberate disobedience. When confronted, he bold-faced denied it. Fortunately, he's still at the young age of innocence where he is unable to comfortably and with full conviction lie. He still has this smirk on his face and he squirms unconfidently. Caught in disobedience and with an attempt to cover his own sin with a lie, now full of shame, he runs and hides. As a daddy, being lied to is one of the most difficult circumstances to navigate for me. I tend to take it personally and have to fight the temptation to respond out of my hurt. When I respond from pain, I

WHAT WAS ONCE OUR SOURCE OF
PLEASURE, ENJOYMENT, CONTENTMENT,
AND SATISFACTION WOULD BECOME THE
SOUL'S DEEPEST CHASM.

find it leads to manipulation, ultimately ending in a manufactured response of, "I'm sorry."

If our children really knew how much we loved them, why would they lie to us?

It's been a difficult lesson for me to learn that when one of my sons sins, he sins against a holy, righteous, and perfect father -- unfortunately, I'm just collateral damage. Reality is, our sin always affects more than just us.

In every sin, we believe the lie that we don't need God -- that we are okay without Him, and we can find fulfillment and satisfaction on our own. It is about believing a lie and chasing after something that is outside of God Himself. That lie always leaves us empty and wanting.

The good news is...
the story doesn't end there.

The beautiful, undeserved grace is that in our emptiness and longing, we begin to understand there is need beyond us and we are not okay without God. We cannot hide from God nor cover our own shame. The truth of the scriptures is that God pursues us in our sin.

May our children come to know the lies of the adversary and may the lies be replaced with the truth of His love.

READ

Genesis 3v1-5; Isaiah 14v12-14; Matthew 4v1; John 8v44, 10v10; 2 Corinthians 11v14-15

MEMORIZE

Everything was good but: everything was about to change.

The most deceitful, crafty, and tricky animal in the garden was: the serpent.

The serpent was: the enemy (Satan means adversary).

The serpent deceived Adam and Eve into thinking that they didn't: need God anymore.

But that wasn't true, was it? – That's called: a lie.

CHAT

Q: How much do we need God? When do we need God? How did you need God today?

A: Always.

Q: What is deception? How are we deceived?

A: The act of making someone believe something that is not true. That's a lie. We are deceived by believing we cannot trust God. Do you struggle to trust God?

Q: What was the lie Satan told Adam and Eve?

A: They didn't need God. They were okay without him. They could be their own God.

Q: What did we learn about God?

A: He is not the adversary. He tells truth, not lies. He is trustworthy.

Q: Where/how do we see the gospel?

A: Deception is everywhere. Our need is great. Jesus is our only hope.

PRAY

God, we are tempted to believe that we do not need You. Every day, at every turn, it is easy to forget that You are good and You alone satisfy our heart's deepest longing. Help us to know and remember that You are our everything. Your love holds everything together. Amen.

EVERYTHING WAS GOOD BUT
EVERYTHING WAS ABOUT TO CHANGE.

THE MOST DECEITFUL, CRAFTY, AND TRICKY ANIMAL IN THE GARDEN WAS
THE SERPENT.
THE SERPENT WAS
THE ENEMY
(SATAN MEANS ADVERSARY).

THE SERPENT DECEIVED ADAM AND EVE INTO THINKING THAT THEY DIDN'T
NEED GOD ANYMORE.

BUT THAT WASN'T TRUE WAS IT? – THAT'S CALLED
A LIE.

07
THE GREAT LIE

But the serpent said to the woman, "You will not surely die."
Genesis 3v4

Unable to overthrow the sovereign King and secure the throne of the Most High, in his defeat, Lucifer, turned-Satan, sought revenge. Satan and his legion of the fallen shifted their desires from God's throne to God's heart. Satan and his army knew intimately that it is God's desire that man and woman would know Him and would be captivated by His love. The enemy knew that the love of the King was too good to reject. The invitation to be with Him and live with Him was too full to ignore. The truth is that mankind was created with an inner compass set to be united with the creator. Creating us out of His fullness, in His likeness, He put the desire for more deep within our DNA. It was God's grand design that we would never be fully satisfied apart from Him and outside of His love.

God's grand design was love.

The truth is that we were designed with an insatiable and relentless desire for love. John writes that "God is love." We are designed for God. Our desire for God is fierce. **God's love for His beloved is ferocious.**

The Bible says that "you will know the truth and the truth will set you free." Satan turns his gaze toward truth and sets out to sabotage love. The tactic is simple: disrupt the longing, deceive the heart, and distort the truth.

"*Did God actually say, 'You shall not eat of any tree in the garden?"* (Genesis 3v1). He commences the sabotage with a question. He tills the ground and readies the soil of the heart for the seed of doubt.

Eve answers, "*We may eat of the fruit of the trees in the garden, but God said, 'You shall not eat of the fruit of the tree that is in the midst of the garden, neither shall you touch it, lest you die"* (Genesis 3v2-3).

Eve knows the truth. She trusts and believes her creator. Satan knows this will not be an easy trap to set. He must move with surgical and swift precision. He knows he has to seduce the beloved to disconnect the heart. He must entice her away.

He weaves a new narrative.

He tells a different story.

He disguises his blood-thirsty roar and sets the trap.

But the serpent said to the woman, "You will not surely die" (Genesis 3v4).

In one fell swoop, the adversary moves from doubt to deception. In a bold act, he calls God a liar. With every breath and every syllable, he wields more power. Hand over hand in a game of tug-of-war, he pulls the woman's heart closer to his. With every tug and each pull, the distance grows between her heart and the heart of her creator. The further she moves away, the more the adversary can move in deeper. His tactic seems to be working.

Given Satan's primal position in the original design of the narrative, he knew that humanity was fashioned with an innate desire for more. Made from the likeness of the sovereign creator and brought to life with His very breath, the adversary would attack there. He would create the illusion of more.

Deception turns to distortion and full-blown manipulation.

The bait is set; the adversary moves to set the hook.

"For God knows that when you eat of it your eyes will be opened, and you will be like God, knowing good and evil" (Genesis 3v5).

He offers the illusion of more. He seduces them with the appearance of control, power, and authority. It arrests their attention and stirs their affections. He weaves the narrative that their trusted creator, their loving and sovereign King, is holding out on them.

They take the bait.

The hook is set.

"So when the woman saw that the tree was good for food, and that it was a delight to the eyes, and that the tree was to be desired to make one wise, she took of its fruit and ate, and she also gave some to her husband who was with her, and he ate" (Genesis 3v6).

They lose trust in their creator and join the ranks of the fallen. In the midst of the beloved's confusion, the creator's love was waiting to be revealed.

Our children join the ranks of the fallen from birth, brought innocent and desperate into this sin-soaked, sin-stained condition with a gravitational pull toward rebellion. Victims of deceit and lovers of more, there is a war waging for their hearts. The adversary spins his tale from the beginning, but the father is still on the move, pursuing, beckoning, calling, renewing His creation. He continues to tell His story and reveal His love.

Talking to our children about the nature of sin can be a difficult thing. We all want our children to have a moral compass that keeps them from the destructive consequences of sin, but there is more beyond behavior. Our sinful nature will wear us down and win over our hearts. The prophet Jeremiah says, "The heart is deceitful above all things, and desperately sick; who can understand it?" (Jeremiah 17v9). We know the only cure or remedy to this indwelling sin is not morality (law), but Christ. He is the answer. The invitation as parents is to prepare our children's hearts, like gardeners, to receive this life-giving good news about Jesus Christ our savior. If we are to cultivate the soil of our children's hearts to beat to the rhythm of God's redemptive plan, then we have to help our children understand sin beyond mere behavior that moves to deep belief.

One of my (David) favorite recent moments was when my wife Tara was out of town and my youngest got caught red-handed throwing a toy in the toilet. The interaction was hilarious. "Moses, did you throw that in the toilet?" His reply: "No daddy, mommy did it." I say, "Really? Mommy threw your toy man in the toilet?" Looking at me with all the confidence of a veteran politician, a simple "yes" comes out of his devious little face. It always baffles me how easy it is for my three-year-old to tell a lie. They can be so illogical.

Our children's struggle with truth-telling in our household has always made me think about how my wife and I conduct ourselves. Over time I have come to the conclusion that we too interact with lies on a daily basis. We both believe and tell lies. Our lies are much more sophisticated and make greater sense than the seemingly illogical lies of my three-year-old, but nonetheless it is a part of our everyday life. As I search the scriptures, I see that at the root, the motivation of both telling and believing lies is self-preservation. We long for joy; we want to experience worth and value. We want to participate in great things. So, in an attempt to quench the hedonism that exists in our hearts, we are willing to say and believe things that are simply not true. As a parent, I talk with my children about telling lies. But more than that, I talk about the dangers of believing them. Our willingness to tell a lie is rooted in our belief in lies. It usually has to do with believing a lie about who God is. If we are to overcome the obstacle of deceit in our own hearts, we must begin by seeing God as trustworthy, unable to lie, and without deceit. As we begin to teach our children about the faithfulness of God, the lies they believe will be exposed and truth will be brought to light. When light pierces the darkness, the enemy will have no place to hide.

May our children come to know the pain of deception and may they rest in the freedom of truth.

READ

Genesis 3v6-7; James 1v13-15; Romans 6v23, 12v1-2; 2 Corinthians 4v4; James 1v22-25

MEMORIZE

Unfortunately, Adam and Eve: believed the lie.
Any time we don't trust and believe in God, that's called: sin.
When we sin, that's called: disobedience.
All of sin is: rebellion.
But God's grand design is: love.

CHAT

Q: Why were Adam and Eve deceived?
A: Connect dots to "more" conversation in the image of God. We always desire more; God is "more," but we are deceived and forget that only God's love can provide, satisfy, and fulfill.

Q: Can we trust God? Do we believe in God's love?
A: Yes. Create the understanding that belief follows trust; the more I believe, the more I will trust. Parents, give a story where trust/belief was difficult for you.

Q: What happens in our disobedience?
A: We love ourselves and/or seek the love of others more than the father, and we seek the satisfaction and fulfillment of other people or objects more than God.

Q: What did we learn about God?
A: He is trustworthy and dependable, and sin is rebellion against Him.

Q: Where/how do we see the gospel?
A: We crave rebellion. God showed His ultimate love through Jesus.

PRAY

God, we are fragile and needy, but You are strong and able. Every day, it is easy to fall into the traps that have been set by the adversary. But, God, You have provided a way around them. May our hearts trust and know that You are good. Your love holds everything together. Amen.

BELIEVED THE

ANYTIME WE DON'T TRUST IN AND BELIEVE IN GOD TH

SIN

WHEN WE SIN, THAT'S CA

DISOBEDIENC

ALL OF SIN

REBELLIO

BUT GOD'S GRAND DESI

LOVE

08
THE SHAME

"We are half-hearted creatures, fooling about with drink and sex and ambition when infinite joy is offered us, like an ignorant child who wants to go on making mud pies in a slum because he cannot imagine what is meant by the offer of a holiday at the sea. We are far too easily pleased."
C. S. Lewis [1]

Then the eyes of both were opened, and they knew that they were naked. And they sewed fig leaves together and made themselves loincloths.
Genesis 3v7

In the great moment of deception, Adam and Eve forgot. They forgot the voice of their creator saying, "This is good... This is very good. You're mine. I love you. I want you. All of you. You will be with me, work with me, create with me. I will provide everything you need. You will find deep meaning in me. I love you. You are mine."

The man and woman lost sight of love.

They were deceived into thinking there was more beyond their creator; deceived into thinking that their primal longings and deep desires could be fulfilled and satisfied outside of intimacy from their God. In the great lie, the man and the woman lost sight of who God is. They forgot that He alone always does what is good, right, and perfect; that He is completely and fully sufficient, in and of Himself; that He is unchanging, completely consistent; that He is holy, righteous and just; that He is powerful and present; that He is matchless in His glory; that He is good, great and provocatively gracious; that He is patient and kind; that He is faithful; that He is magnificent, full of splendor and awe; that He is king; that He is a promise maker and promise keeper; that He is father. As a perfect father, He provides, protects, and is perfectly present with His family. He loves with perfect precision; nothing is ever outside of our good, and everything is always for His glory. He has adopted us as his own and reminds us that, "you are mine."

He is love. He loves with a stubborn love... A covenant-keeping, grace-filled, never-leaving, without-an-exit-strategy kind of love.

Adam and Eve forgot that He was the one who created the fruit. He was the one who made it look lovely, pleasing to the eye, and made it wildly delicious to the taste. All this to remind them of His insanely provocative and scandalous grace. Adam and Eve were deceived into thinking that their deepest needs and wildest yearnings could be met beyond the hand of their creator.

The narrative tailspins out of control; the lie embeds deeper and infests the whole story. "You must try harder, work more, accumulate, amass, consume. Your performance will prove your worth!"

The enemy weaves the new storyline: *ignore the longing beneath the longing; forget the yearning for more; disregard the desire under the desire. God cannot satisfy. You cannot trust Him to hold your heart and protect you.* Enticed away from the heart of our God, life is lived on the circumference and edges where the lies to continue to mount. "He isn't, he can't, he won't, he's holding out on you, he's absent. Where was your God when you needed Him most?" So we look some other place, go elsewhere, convince ourselves that we are not wandering aimlessly. Over and over, we recite, "I have this all under control."

This is how sin works.

Sin promises that the thirst will be quenched, yet we are thirstier still. It promises fulfillment, yet emptiness abounds. It promises wisdom but leaves us in folly. It promises wholeness yet leaves destruction in its wake. The great lie says that we can be our own gods, that we can ascend the mount of the most high, but we end up in the pigpen as beggars in complete desperation. The liar says that this is the way to freedom, but bondage swells.

The voice that says, "You are mine, you are special and unique, filled with the image of your creator, you are full of beauty and wonder, insanely curious to always remember there is more in me, stay close and remain intimate, there is complete freedom with me," is replaced with the voice that screams, "You came from nothing and to nothing you will return, you are a mistake, full of shame, no one wants you, you're on your own now. Good luck out there."

Sin has ravaged our entire being. We've forgotten who we are; we've even forgotten how to remember who we are. Now, full of shame, forced deeper into hiding, we pursue remedies to cover our own sin and shame.

"And they heard the sound of the LORD God walking in the garden in the cool of the day, and the man and his wife hid themselves from the presence of the LORD God among the trees of the garden."
Genesis 3v8

It doesn't matter how many proverbial fig leaves we sew together, or how deeply into the forest we seek refuge; we know we will never be able to cover our shame or outrun our unbelief. It has become a part of who we are. Sin has birthed death. And the consequences will be greater than ever imagined.

But love will never stop pursuing.

Love will be the covering once again.

Even lured abroad to a life apart from God, innately we never stop searching for Him. Eden is always calling. Our creator God is always searching, always revealing, always provocatively gracious.

I (David) have struggled with shame language my whole life. I grew up around a lot of manipulative people that taught me early how to use shame to motivate. I have allowed shame to motivate many different aspects of my life. I've been tempted in many situations to hide my radical past in an attempt to make myself look like something I am not. As a result of my past experience, I found myself using shame to correct my children's behavior. When I reread Genesis 2 with gospel lenses, I realized how opposite this tactic of discipline was to the image of our father that I was so desperately trying to convey. God never used shame to interact with His beloved. At the core of who God is, we see only Truth and Love at work together to redeem that which was broken. Not only did God exclude shame, but He covered our guilt and shame by sacrificing His own creation. We know now that this first sacrifice foreshadowed how He would cover our guilt and shame through the sacrifice of Christ.

Over the last couple of years, I have worked hard to remove shame language when I discipline my children for their sinful actions and attitudes. Instead, I attempt to shepherd them in truth and love. I always try to remember that my goal is not to modify their behavior so they reflect well on me, but rather to nurture their hearts so that they would be reconciled to the Father. This isn't always easy, and it is impossible to do in the flesh. Most of my effort is spent crying out to the Lord for help. I need to be reminded daily of my identity in Christ, that I am His beloved and have been invited into His full inheritance. It is only then that I am able to extend to my children the same invitation the Father extends to me. I sacrifice my own flesh so I can cover their guilt in shame in Truth and Love. That's called grace.

When our children lose sight of love, when they are caught in disobedience and unbelief, that's the moment to pursue them, to seek them out, to remind them who the father is, what he has done, and what he is doing. To remind them whose they are. They are His; He loves them; He wants them.

May we learn to pursue our children as Christ pursues us.

READ

Genesis 3v8-1; Psalm 38v1-10; 2 Corinthians 12v9-10; 1 Corinthians 15v34, Isaiah 55v6; Psalm 130v4, 1 John 1v9, Galatians 5v1

MEMORIZE

Remember, there is always freedom in: love and obedience.
But Adam and Eve: disobeyed.
All sin produces: shame and separation.
When we sin, we hurt the heart of God: because God loves us.
So Adam and Eve tried to: cover their own shame.

CHAT

Q: Why is there freedom in obedience and not in disobedience?
A: There is freedom in trust and love. Adam and Eve believed a lie. There is no love in a lie.

Q: What happens when people tell lies? How you feel when people lie to you or you lie to them?
A: People get hurt. Trust is broken. We try to hide our shame and cover our own sin.

Q: What happens when we sin?
A: We hurt God's heart. There is no freedom in sin. Adam and Eve felt shame, so they hid and tried to cover their own shame.

Q: What did we learn about God?
A: God pursues Adam and Eve in their sin. Pursuit is love.

Q: Where/how do we see the gospel?
A: God pursued extravagantly through the cross, covered our sin, and brought freedom again.

PRAY

God, You love us with a fierce, strong, limitless love that will go to any length to remind us that we are Yours. Forgive us for the pain we cause Your heart as we look away from You in search of who we are elsewhere. Thank you that Your love is bigger than our unbelief and that Your love holds everything together. Amen.

NOW REMEMBER, THERE IS ALWAYS FREEDOM IN
LOVE AND OBEDIENCE.

BUT ADAM AND EVE
DISOBEYED.

ALL SIN PRODUCES
SHAME AND SEPERATION.

WHEN WE SIN, WE HURT THE HEART OF GOD
BECAUSE GOD LOVES US.

SO ADAM AND EVE TRIED TO
COVER THEIR OWN SHAME.

09
THE CONSEQUENCE

"But the LORD God called to the man and said to him, 'Where are you?' And he said, 'I heard the sound of you in the garden, and I was afraid, because I was naked, and I hid myself.' He said, 'Who told you that you were naked?'"
Genesis 3v9-11

Adam and Eve took the bait and took the bite, and everything changed. Since that tragic moment of rebellion in the garden of Eden, found in the opening pages of scripture, humanity has been in a constant pursuit of discovery and connection, trying once again to know its identity... trying to find its story. Things are not as they should be.

The song of creation and the Father's love is all around us, filling every nook and cranny. It reminds us of more and stirs our affections. It's a song with which we are all familiar, like a lullaby sung to us night after night as a child. It holds a sense of nostalgia, a sense of home. The unmistakable atmosphere of freedom, safety, care, and provision. But the adversary follows behind, lurking in the shadows, distorting and manipulating, spinning his own version of the story.

We awaken to the reality of the fall.

Pain replaced blessing. Tears replaced comfort. Neglect where there was relief. Bruised and torn for whole and complete. Brokenness in place of peace. Isolation displaced family. Pleasure swapped with agony. Pride in place of humility. Longing where there was once contentment. Doubt moved in where belief once lived.

Naked.
> *Hiding.*
>> *Blaming.*
>>> *Suffering.*
>>>> *Wandering.*
>>>>> *Bound.*
>>>>>> **Full of Shame.**

Where Adam and Eve once walked in complete bliss and in shame-less, naked freedom, they attempt to cover their own nakedness and find covering among the trees. The serpent had promised them a bigger role in the story and had convinced them they could experience more beyond the relationship of their God. Disobedience hurts. Injustice cuts deeply. But the father, the creator of everything, pursues. The innocent who was wronged, the faithful who was betrayed, the lover who was rejected for lovers less wild, pursued. He searched, He sought, He knew... And with a broken heart, He went to Adam and Eve.

Have you eaten of the tree of which I commanded you not to eat?"
"The man said, "The woman whom you gave to be with me, she gave me fruit of the tree, and I ate." Then the LORD God said to the woman, "What is this that you have done?" The woman said, "The serpent deceived me, and I ate."
Genesis 3v12-13

Attempting to cover their own nakedness and hiding among the trees, now they blame. There seems to be some dispute over whether Adam was present for the great lie. Was Adam there, close by, watching his wife Eve being tempted by the enemy? Was the man passively beside his Eve, witnessing the seduction of his wife's heart away from truth?

It would seem that in order to confess, "She gave me fruit of the tree, and I ate," Adam would have had to have been inconspicuously near the events that unfurled, if not intimately near. He forfeited his leadership and call to protect, and now he spinelessly points his finger at his creator and simultaneously at Eve and says, "It's not my fault." Eve responds in one part confession and the other part blame, muttering, "I was deceived and wooed by the serpent."

The central revelation in the moment of deception was clear: humanity didn't trust the heart of the creator and looked elsewhere for satisfaction. Any time we don't trust and believe God, that's called sin. All of sin is an act of hostile rebellion against a perfect God. Consequence ensues.

No one escapes the rebellion unscathed. The enemy strikes a significant blow, but the righteous, all-powerful king promises a time when he will land the final, decisive blow. God declares to Satan his future demise. There will be no final victory for the enemy. The king will prevail.

God is holy, righteous, and perfect. Because He is set apart, He cannot allow sin to remain in His presence. Adam and Eve became sinners, victims to the wily and cunning scheme of the enemy. With a broken heart and in a provocative act of grace, the Holy Father clothes the man's and the woman's nakedness with garments made from the skin of animals, an act that would ultimately foreshadow an ultimate and complete covering for humanity. Then He sends them away from His presence. God banishes them from the place that flourished and blossomed with life due to His presence. Eden, the garden of life that was created to perfectly provide union, and remind humanity of the creator and their need for him became impenetrable. God would place cherubim at the entrance of garden to keep sin out and remind Satan of the place from which he had fallen.

The consequence was a finite and fragile life lived outside of perfection. Humanity would have to work, create, and bear children in an exhausting, painful, struggle-filled life. They were reminded of their frail and fragile origins. Made from the dust of the ground, they were promised "to dust you shall return" (Genesis 3v19).

Things were not as they should be.

I (Freddy) have two boys. One naturally hides, and the other naturally blames. Both tell lies in an attempt to right a wrong or fix the cracks. Embarrassed, caught, self-protective, they lose sight of love. We've forgotten "You're mine. I love you. I want you... all of you." When caught in disobedience and unbelief, that's the moment to pursue them, to seek them out, to remind them who the father is, what He has done, and what He is doing. To remind them whose they are. They are His; He loves them; He wants them. That is the moment to stir the deep waters of their hearts.

As the deer pants for the water brooks,
So my soul pants for You, O God.
My soul thirsts for God, for the living God;
When shall I come and appear before God.
Psalm 42v1-2

A few years ago I had to walk through an incident with my youngest son. When I asked him what happened, he went on to share about the events that unfolded upstairs. Ultimately we arrived in the space where he felt embarrassed so he lied in an attempt to cover his shame. As we worked through the consequences of disobedience we were reminded that we have been given the gift of grace even though we don't deserve it, but unfortunately there are still consequences to our sin. There are always consequences to sin. I asked him what the consequence was in the garden for Adam and Eve's disobedience. He said, "God removed them from the garden." I asked him why? He said, "Because of their sin." I started the sentence, "All disobedience is..."—"Sin," he finished. At that moment, with his eye brows furled, his forehead wrinkled, and a deep grimace on his face, he said, "So God is gonna remove me, daddy?" I replied, "Unfortunately buddy, God has already removed you from His presence; in fact He has removed all of us. We are all sinners, unable to save ourselves and be with Him." My son began to cry and with a heart full of sadness and shame, he said, "God doesn't love me anymore." I said, "Buddy, the story doesn't end there... that's the good news. God's love is bigger and better than our sin. Jesus came to rescue us so we could know Him and be with Him again."

Our actions have consequences. It has been an unforeseen gift to learn and understand as a family the freedom that comes with love and obedience and the adverse as well -- no freedom in disobedience. Understanding this early in life is a very healthy truth for our children to grasp. It will preserve them and keep them safe. But ultimately we know that eternal safety only comes when our children find themselves in the arms of God. Our sin not only has earthly consequences, but more gravely, it separates us from the one place we actually experience life -- the presence of God. *The ultimate goal in teaching our children about the consequences of their actions is not safety but rather redemption.* What good is a safe and quiet life that has not been restored, that has not been saved from the consequences of sin and restored into the life of the Father? Disobedience is an incredible opportunity to discuss the consequences of sin. God created us out of love and for His glory. His desire is for His glory and our good. The consequences of sin actually separate us from an all-encompassing good. Sin separates us from the very love we so desperately desire and a belonging that goes beyond anything we have ever known. We do not want our children ultimately to fear

WE LOST SIGHT OF LOVE.

consequence but rather *to long for God*.

May the longing in our children's heart reveal the depth of the Father's love.

READ

Genesis 3v12-24; Isiah 59v2, Romans 5v12, 6v23, Ephesians 2v1, 2
Thessalonians 1v9

MEMORIZE

Because Adam and Eve sinned: everything changed.
Adam and Eve: forgot.
God is holy and always does what is: good, right, and perfect.
Because God is holy, He does not allow: sin to be in His presence.
God punished Adam and Eve by: removing them from the garden
(His presence).

CHAT

Q: When Adam and Eve sinned, what changed?
A: Everything! What specifically? Before sin, there was freedom; they weren't
hiding. Now they're hiding and full of shame. Hiding and then blaming.

Q: What specific consequences did God give Adam and Eve?
A: Ultimately, sin separates us from God, so God removed them from the
garden... The place of God's protection, provision, and presence.

Q: Why does God remove them from the garden / His presence?
A: He is holy and does not allow sin to be in His presence.

Q: What did we learn about God?
A: He is holy, righteous, and perfect. God takes sin seriously, because He
loves us.

Q: Where/how do we see the gospel?
A: Our sin separates us from God, but God's love is bigger and better than
sin. He pursued us and brought us close again through His son Jesus and His
work on the cross.

PRAY

God, our sin separates us from You. When we don't trust You, we put our
hope in other people and other things. May we truly know that sin always
brings distance from You and leaves us empty, wanting more. Help us to
know that our hearts can never truly delight in anything other than being
with You. And thank you that Your love holds everything together. Amen.

EVERYTHING CHANGED

ADAM AND EVE

FORGOT

GOD IS HOLY AND ALWAYS DOES WHAT

GOOD, RIGHT
AND PERFECT

BECAUSE GOD IS HOLY, HE DOES NOT ALLO

SIN TO BE IN HIS PRESENC

SO GOD PUNISHED ADAM AND EVE

REMOVING THEM FROM THE GARD

HIS PRESENCE

10
THE DESPERATION

Their communion broken, driven from the presence of God and the home God had created for them, Adam and Eve's life outside the garden was anything but blissful. They were not okay with God. Humanity would have to live in constant and continual neediness.

There is story in the book of Luke, about a wayward, rebellious son. The story opens with the younger of two sons demanding that his father give him his inheritance now. This is essentially to say, "I wish you were dead now, so I can have what is rightfully mine." Discontented in his situation, everything he had with his father and all that would be his one day wasn't good enough for the son.

He wanted more.

Unwilling to be patient and await the gift that would one day be his, he took his newly acquired inheritance and set sail to a distant land to chase the desires deep within his heart. The scriptures tell us that he squandered all that he had in reckless living. Enticed away, in an effort to live in freedom and pursue what he believed would bring him fulfillment, the son lost everything. At that very time, a great famine swept through the land. The wandering son had nothing, and in complete desperation, he took a job far beneath his dignity, religion, and place in society. Working for a foreigner in a distant land, he would be responsible to feed the man's pigs.

While working in the fields in the heat of the day with nothing to fill his belly, hoping for some of the leftover food the pigs hadn't eaten and with nothing to quench his thirst, the son began dreaming of days past. He remembered who he once was and all that he had in his father's house as one of his sons. Every need was fully met by his father. He began to smile, thinking back on all the memories; as a child, he was unable to hold his father's whole hand. With his small hand swallowed up in the bigness of his father's, he could only grip one finger and hold tight. He remembered his father's ring and the symbol that represented the seal of his family, as they walked the property sharing stories and overlooking all that his father had been blessed with. He remembered hearing his father's deep tenor voice in his head, explaining that one day all this would belong to him and his brother. "Why?" the son asked. His father went on to explain that, simply because he was his father's son, all that his father had would be his. The son knew who he was because of who the father was. As he grew in age and stature, the son would watch how his father managed and looked over all he had. He watched closely how the father treated his servants with dignity and respect and how they cherished the father because of it. They would do anything for him without even the slightest grumble. The father made them feel as if they were part of the family. The father would teach the two sons how to work hard and join him in his work.

The son wakes to the reality of his fall.

He remembers the height from which he has fallen.

At rock bottom, the son remembers. He remembers that his father has more than enough, that even his servants are filled and there is plenty left. He knows home is his only option. He must return back to his father. His appetite more insatiable than before, his longing more evident, he sets out for home.

The longing brought him home.

"And he arose and came to his father. But while he was still a long way off, his father saw him and felt compassion, and ran and embraced him and kissed him."
Luke 15v20

The greater barrier to love is ego, the life of the self. In long term suffering, if you don't give in to self pity, slowly, almost imperceptibly, self dies. This death of the self offers ideal growing conditions for love."
Paul Miller [2]

According to daily routine, the faithful father made his rounds at dusk, making sure the daily work was wrapping up and preparations for tomorrow's labor were in place. It was intentional space created for his heart to reflect, commune, and thank God for all that He had provided. He ended his rounds at the high point on the front side of the property that overlooked the road leading up to the house. It was there every evening that he prayed for his youngest son. Most nights he lingered a bit longer, always hopeful that just maybe this could be the night his son returned. He often replayed the scene from that dreadful day the son voiced those hateful words, turned his back, and walked out. Nonetheless, the faithful father never stopped searching, hoping, waiting, weeping.

It was that hour of the evening, the sun just beginning to set. The father had finished his rounds for the evening and found himself in that familiar place, looking out, peering in the distance. After lingering for a few moments longer, the father breathed in deep and turned back toward the house. But this night, the longing felt heavier. After a few steps, he stopped. Turning back toward the high point overlooking the front of his property, he saw something far in the distance. Unable to clearly make out the silhouette in the dimly lit sky, he stepped closer. "I know that posture. I know that gait," the father thought. He recognized the strut of the figure. He always told his younger son to stand up straight and stop hunching over. It was a bit of swagger mixed with poor posture.

What is that?
Who is...?
Could it be...?
Is that my...?

He couldn't finish his thoughts before he began to run. Overwhelmed with compassion and filled with joy, he rolled his robe up past his knees and ran toward his son. Who knows the last time the old man ran, but he couldn't stop, he was compelled to go to his son. While awkwardly running, so as not to trip over his rolled up robe, the father continually shouted, "My son! My son! My son is home!" in the deep tenor that the son knew so well. The son stopped in his tracks as his father ran toward him. He lunged, nearly tackling the wayward young man in a full embrace. Reminiscent of childhood, the father lifted the son into the air so his feet were no longer touching the ground beneath him. The prodigal felt his embrace and the kiss upon his cheek.

Overwhelmed, the son could not contain his brokenness. He broke at his father's feet. He wept, struggling to speak the words through the pain and tears.

"Father, I'm sorry. I'm sorry. I'm sorry... I'm no longer worthy to be your son. I've sinned against God and against you. I am no longer worthy to be called your son. I'm sorry. I've disgraced our family. I've disappointed you. I'm sorry. I've returned home to beg Your pardon and become one of Your servants"

"I am your father. You are my son. You are mine."

The soft yet strong timbre of the father's voice was unmistakable.

"Son, you are home again."

But the father said to his servants, 'Bring quickly the best robe, and put it on him, and put a ring on his hand, and shoes on his feet. And bring the fattened calf and kill it, and let us eat and celebrate. For this my son was dead, and is alive again; he was lost, and is found.' And they began to celebrate.
Luke 15v22-24

The faithful father rolled out the red carpet for his lost son. The father went to great lengths to remind his son of who he is. The son's brokenness was met with provocative grace. "Servant? No. You are my son!" They stood at ground zero for what makes love possible. Desperation, repentance, return, and grace. Now humility sets in. The love of the father, was so deep that he let his beloved son go. He knew and trusted that love would be good enough to bring him home. The heart had become fertile for identity to set. The father gave his son a robe, a ring bearing the mark of the family, sandals, a fattened calf. "My son is alive. My son is home."

And I am sure of this, that he who began a good work in you will bring it to completion at the day of Jesus Christ.
Philippians 1v6

Though your sins are as scarlet, they will be as white as snow. Though they are red like crimson, they will be like wool.
Isaiah 1v18

Outside of the garden, no longer beneath the creator's wings of protection, where perfect provision met neediness, the man and the woman struggle. Eden still in their rear view mirror—with all of its memories, all of its perfection—felt so close, but it might as well have been an eternity away. There was no going back. They turned their backs on their creator, so they had to live with the consequences with every day that passed as the man and woman aged. As they started a family of their own, ebbing and flowing between struggle caused by sin and pleasure brought by grace, they would never stop longing for Eden. There would never be contentment apart from their God.

But the story doesn't end here.

God never stops pursuing His beloved.

As parents, we desire obedience from our children. After all, obedience is a biblical command, right? We are still living outside of Eden, and disobedience is painful. The older our children become, the more painfully and acutely we feel the rejection. The harsher their words become and the louder their voices raise, the more readily we try to fix and control. If our children grow up being taught that they've sinned against us, they will grow up learning to please us rather than learning to love us.

I (Freddy) had a conversation recently with a mother who now has grown children. Several of her children, after being "raised in church," have since walked away from the church and from the God they knew in their youth. Heartbroken, confused, she now realizes how much she idolized her children when they were young. This unfortunate story prevails in our country. For a lot of parents, it's easy to pour everything into our children. But if we're not careful, in an attempt to love and serve, we can begin to idolize our children.

The pursuit of our children takes the place of our pursuit of God.

Our children grow up trying to meet our expectations, known and unknown, subtle and overt, without ever truly understanding obedience outside of obligation. They will grow up thinking that we are only proud of what they do and accomplish, and they will feel shame in poor performance and lesser achievements. This further entrenches and enforces the cultural push toward comparison.

This is the world I grew up in -- heavy-laden with expectations. It was by no fault of anyone, anything, or any institution specifically -- It's the world we live in. I learned young and subconsciously that disappointment is not fun. Since disappointment comes from unmet expectations, I became adept at adapting to the expectations surrounding me. I didn't want to let anyone down.

The scary reality is that this world formed at an innate and primal depth. This was subterranean, lurking beneath the surface. Recently, I have begun to notice the same tendencies in my oldest son. The other day, he told me that he didn't feel good enough. He's a feeler (a Meyers-Briggs reference), meaning that he naturally feels his way through life. He feels the demands at school and the comparisons with his friends. He knows the Disney narrative and the celebration of skin-deep beauty. He genuinely wants to do well but he has to fight the tendency to perform. He responds well to challenges and competition -- he seeks to achieve and conquer, all of which are great qualities that I deeply admire in him, but obedience flows from love, not performance. There is only true freedom in obedience. True freedom flows from a place of love and acceptance that only Christ can provide for us.

From the time we can remember, we tried to shape and form his base identity apart from performance. "Mommy and daddy are proud of you... Just because of who you are. You are our son... And because you are our son, we love you. Nothing can ever make us love you more or less. YOU ARE MY SON."

Grace is God throwing His arms around us and saying,

> *"You are mine."*

> *"I want you."*

May our children come to find the desperation as an invitation into more.

READ

Genesis 3v21-24; Psalm 42v1-2, 50v15, 91v14-16; Romans 3v23, 5v12-19; Isaiah 59v1-2; John 4v18

MEMORIZE

Adam and Eve were now: sinners.
As hard as they tried, Adam and Eve could not fix: what was broken.
They never stopped: needing God.
And God would never stop: loving them.
But the story doesn't: end there.

CHAT

Q: What does it mean to be a sinner?
A: It means that we need God. We crave rebellion. Our brokenness shows our need for God.

Q: Are there moments when we feel the need for God more? What are some of those moments?
A: We always need God. We never stop needing him, especially in moments of unbelief.

Q: When we sin and go our own way, does God stop loving us?
A: No. Our sin reminds us that we need God. He pursues.

Q: What did we learn about God?
A: We see that grace from the father covers nakedness and brokenness.

Q: Where/how do we see the gospel?
A: The covering of their nakedness foreshadowed the way the father would ultimately cover all sin with the perfect, shed blood of Jesus.

PRAY

God, thank you for the gentle and tender, and at times sharp and deep, reminders that we are always in need of You. Thank you that over and over, You lavish us with Your deep love and affection. God, help us in our unbelief to remember Your goodness and to know Your nearness. Thank you that Your love holds everything together. Amen.

ADAM AND EVE WERE NOW
SINNERS.
AS HARD AS THEY TRIED, ADAM AND EVE COULD NOT FIX
WHAT WAS BROKEN.
THEY NEVER STOPPED
NEEDING GOD.
AND GOD WOULD NEVER STOP
LOVING THEM.
BUT THE STORY DOESN'T
END THERE.

GOSPEL

THE GREAT RESCUE
GRACE
HOLINESS
JESUS IS BETTER
BELONGING

...but God shows his love for us in that while we were still sinners, Christ died for us.
Romans 5v8

For our sake he made him to be sin who knew no sin, so that in him we might become the righteousness of God.
2 Corinthians 5v21

A COVENANT IS A COMMITMENT; IT'S AN UNCONDITIONAL, UNBREAKABLE, NEVER-ENDING, ALWAYS-AND-FOREVER KIND OF COMMITMENT. THAT'S WHO GOD IS. HE IS FAITHFUL.

Disobedience hurts. Injustice cuts deeply. But the Father, the creator of everything, pursues. The innocent who was wronged, the faithful who was betrayed, the lover who was rejected for lovers less wild, pursued. He searched, He sought, He knew... And with a broken heart, He went to Adam and Eve.

"You are mine. I want you. All of you."

God would make a new promise with His people; out of His faithfulness, not theirs, God would make good on His promise. God would always continue to provide perfectly for His children.

Though God's people would run from Him and go through droughts of forgetting Him, their God would never stop loving them and they would never stop needing Him. Though they would wander, He would remind them of His promise and bring them back home. Though their enemies would triumph, He would rescue them. He promised He would be the shepherd they needed most and that He would provide perfectly for them. He would be their father and He would be their home.

This truth was a promise God made to his people. This promise was called a covenant. It's beyond a contract, more than an exchange of "I cross my heart and hope to die," more than a mere agreement. A covenant is a commitment; it's an unconditional, unbreakable, never-ending, always-and-forever kind of commitment. That's who God is. He is faithful.

*'I will look on you with favor and make you fruitful and increase your numbers, and I will keep my covenant with you. You will still be eating last year's harvest when you will have to move it out to make room for the new. I will put my dwelling place among you, and I will not abhor you. **I will walk among you and be your God, and you will be my people**. I am the LORD your God, who brought you out of Egypt so that you would no longer be slaves to the Egyptians; I broke the bars of your yoke and enabled you to walk with heads held high.*
Leviticus 23v9-13

After we have been deceived by distorted truth, God sets out to remind us who He is and what He has done and what He continues to do. Most provocatively, He shows Himself and the extent of His bottomless, unconditional love through His son Jesus. Like the father of the prodigal, He runs to us, wraps His children in a robe, puts a ring on our finger and sandals on our feet.

Love pursues...love engages.

My son has returned HOME.

GOSPEL catechism traces five main parts of the love story of Jesus: **THE GREAT RESCUE, GRACE, HOLINESS, JESUS IS BETTER, BELONGING.**

11
THE GREAT RESCUE

"There is not a square inch in the whole domain of our human existence over which Christ, who is Sovereign over all, does not cry, Mine!"
Abraham Kuyper [1]

...but God shows his love for us in that while we were still sinners, Christ died for us.
Romans 5v8

From the beginning, the divine community (God the Father, God the Son, and God the Holy Spirit) created humanity unique. "You are mine" was the refrain. Unlike the rest of creation, they were invited to reflect Him, to be with Him, work with Him, and join Him in His work. God created a world, placed humanity in it, and provided perfectly everything they needed. But Adam and Eve were deceived by the great lie, and the creator God removed them from His presence. They severed their perfect relationship with God. They lost sight of love.

But the story doesn't end there.

The story of Adam and Eve is the story of humanity. This is our story: a constant seduction of lovers less wild; an insatiable desire for more, a desire that both pushes and pulls our hearts and minds in various untamed trajectories. The adversary continues to weave this new narrative into the hearts and minds of humanity.

The distance continues to grow between humanity and the heart of its creator. God allowed humanity to wander as far as necessary to remember the longing, to remember they were created for more. Like the prodigal son, the longing brought them back to the heart of their faithful father. He never stopped pursuing. He would never stop loving. God would never stop revealing His character and nature, never ceasing to put His glory on display. But lurking close behind, always full of deceit, the enemy was never far, ready to pounce and devour. The closer humanity returned to God, the more lies the enemy spewed. With more proximity came more temptation.

This was the rhythm of humanity for generations and generations, vacillating between deep devotion to God and corrupt pursuits of the heart. Deceit led to distance and truth led back to intimacy again.

By Genesis 12, God had chosen Abram and his descendants, the Israelites, to be a people who would be distinct. God made a promise to Abram. This promise is called a covenant. He promised they would be His people and He would be their God. "You are mine" was the father's refrain. God's intent was to bless them, and they in turn would bless the world. By this promise, the world would know who God was, and what He was like through His people. They would bear His image and reveal His glory to the world. God would once again invite humanity to join Him on His mission to make all things new.

For I am not ashamed of the gospel, for it is the power of God for salvation to everyone who believes...
Romans 1v16

Behold, the days are coming, declares the LORD, when I will make a new covenant with the house of Israel and the house of Judah.
Jeremiah 31v31

Unfortunately, like Adam and Eve, God's people would continue to be corrupted by sin. The adversary would continue to seduce them away from God and distort his truth. They would lose sight of love over and over again, ultimately turning their backs in rebellion, living how they thought was best to live. The adversary's tactic has never changed from the day of the great lie: distort the truth and seduce the beloved into thinking they can find fulfillment and satisfaction outside of the one true God. The repercussions are the same...

Brokenness.
       Hiding.
            Blaming.
                  Suffering.
                        Wandering.
                              Bondage.
                                    Full of Shame.

The story and history of God's people continues along these lines for the rest of the Old Testament. Repentance and proximity to deceit and distance. Return and intimacy to slavery and exile. Belief and trust to doubt and rebellion.

"There is no reason to mince words. I believe that Christianity happens when men and women experience the reckless, raging confidence that comes from knowing the God of Jesus Christ."
Brennan Manning [2]

While we were unable to save ourselves, the great rescue would accomplish everything that was necessary to reconcile humanity back to God. God made a promise, and the faithful father always keeps His promises. Nothing is ever outside His hand, and everything always falls under His sovereign reign and rule. From the first words spoken in creation, through every rebellious attempt to thwart love, God has never ceased to put His glory on display. In every moment there is an act of grace, in every circumstance, a glimpse of more. He promised He would provide perfectly for His children. Out of His great mercy and scandalous grace, God entered into the human condition and the depravity of the human experience to pave the way back home. The perfect provision found in the great rescue reestablishes hope. God the father sends his son Jesus to be with us and invites us back to be with Him. The great rescue reestablishes humanity's communion with God.

This is the gospel.
This is the great rescue.
This is perfect provision.
Jesus is more.

"The story doesn't end there..."

That little phrase has so much meaning. The reality is that we need rescue! We need help from outside of ourselves, someone to come in and deliver us from this body of death (Romans 7v24). The greatest lie is self-sufficiency, that somehow we have a sense of control and if we work hard enough and long enough, we can accomplish all that is necessary to achieve. Of course, we want our children to grow to un-

THERE IS HOPE.

THERE IS MORE.

THERE IS RESCUE.

derstand the beautiful gift of hard work and the grace given to them to provide practically and physically for their families, how to identify and steward that which God has given them, to work from their identity in the gospel and not for their identity. That is a beautiful responsibility, to prepare them like arrows to be shot out. We do not want our children to grow up and be codependent leeches. In the maturation journey, there has to come a moment in which they realize that they cannot rescue themselves from the nature of their own sin. Before they will be willing to follow Christ into eternal freedom, they have to realize their need for rescue in the first place. Getting my (David) children to this point in their life is my greatest desire. Paul talks about wrestling with sin. He says, "Why do I do the things I don't want to do, and the things I know I ought to do, I simply don't do them?" He then belts out the most important question any of us can ask: "Who will deliver me from this body of death?" This is exactly where we want to find our hearts. That is the great paradox of humanity. Created for more, we long for more and are insatiably driven toward more, yet we are completely unable to achieve more on our own. We are wholly desperate and needy. When we come to the realization that we do not have the ability to deliver ourselves from ourselves, then this truth will be like soothing salve for our children's souls: "The story doesn't end there..."

There is hope.

There is more.

There is rescue.

May our children grow to know that God's love is bigger and better than our sin.

READ

Ephesians 2v8-9, 3v18, Colossians 1v15; Hebrews 1v3; John 1v14; Romans 5v1-6, 8v1; 2 Corinthians 5v14-21

MEMORIZE

God's love is: bigger and better than sin.
God would never stop: pursuing His creation (us).
God's love story is about: Jesus.
God's love story about Jesus is called: the gospel.
The gospel means that Jesus came to: rescue us.

CHAT

Q: Who is Jesus?
A: God's son. Theologically, God the Son (a member of the trinity/Godhead).

Q: Why did God have to send Jesus to rescue us? What does Jesus rescue us from?
A: We cannot rescue ourselves. Jesus rescues us from sin, death, and separation. (James 1v15, Romans 6v23)

Q: Why does God continue pursuing humanity?
A: For his glory and out of his glory, He loves. He makes brokenness whole again.

Q: What did we learn about God?
A: His love is big. He makes things new. He pursues because His love is bigger/better than sin.

Q: Where/how do we see the gospel?
A: This is the gospel: God, in his sovereignty, sent his son Jesus to make peace on our behalf. He justified us before the perfect father, and he reconciled us to himself. He has power to save.

PRAY

God, Your love is full and Your love is big. It consumes me and overwhelms me. Out of Your perfect love, You wrote a perfect love story and put Your son Jesus at the center of it. Because of Your great, engulfing love, rescue is possible through Your son Jesus. From the very beginning, You have had us in mind as a part of Your story which shows Your glory. Your love holds everything together. Amen.

GOD'S LOVE IS **BIGGER AND BETTER THAN SIN.**

GOD WOULD NEVER STOP **PURSUING HIS CREATION (US).**

GOD'S LOVE STORY IS ABOUT **JESUS.**

GOD'S LOVE STORY ABOUT JESUS IS CALLED **THE GOSPEL.**

THE GOSPEL MEANS THAT JESUS CAME TO **RESCUE US.**

12
GRACE

And this is eternal life, that they know You the only true God, and Jesus Christ whom You have sent.
John 17v3

After the great lie, everything changed. Trust broken, this perfect relationship was fractured. Our sin severed our relationship with God. But God's love is bigger and better than sin. He promised He would be the shepherd His people needed most. He promised His love is bigger and better than anything that attempts to stir the affections of our heart other than Him. He told The Church that they were like His bride, that He would clothe her in perfection and beauty, adorned in white. He would be standing at the end of the aisle, waiting for her, inviting her, beckoning her.

Jesus arrives on the scene of the New Testament in the first century into a diverse matrix of perspectives. God had been silent from His people for the four-hundred-year intertestamental period between the prophetic writings of Malachi and the opening of Matthew. A birth announcement of a baby born in accordance with the scriptures spread throughout the land. This baby boy, named Jesus, was said to hold prophetic significance for the nation of Israel, God's chosen people. It was written that he would be the promised One, the Son of God, sent to rescue his people from oppression, slavery, and exile. It was clear; God's silence was over.

As we open the pages of the New Testament, the Roman Empire ruled the known world. Riddled with Greek influence from the past reign, the world was dominated by Roman and Greek philosophies. But make no mistake, Caesar was king! No one crossed Rome in conflict and lived to tell about it. The Roman government was ruthless toward anyone or anything that stood in opposition. Simply put, "Oppose Rome and die."

Word continued to slowly and seemingly insignificantly spread about the prophetic nature of the birth of Messiah. Jesus grew up in a sense of obscurity and an even deeper sense of normality. At roughly thirty years old, what was obscure and ambiguous turned clear and HiDef. Jesus was baptized by His cousin John. This act inaugurated Jesus's public ministry. It was then that Jesus called His first disciples and began to preach and teach about the coming kingdom of God.

God would completely and perfectly fulfill His redemptive plan and rescue mission through His son Jesus. Jesus was sent to be with His people, to show the father's love and once and for all bring them close again. God said that He would be their God and they were His people. In His holiness, God does not allow sin to remain in His presence, and in order for humanity to be with Him, the people would need to be sinless. That's our problem; we are sinners, unable to clean ourselves and find our way home. Jesus, full of mercy and abounding grace, proclaims that we cannot, but He can; He has. Jesus, in His majesty and sovereign rule, substituted His righteousness for our sin. In the greatest act of love the world has ever seen, Jesus took our place in death and gave us His life. Because of His perfect righteousness, the father God now looks at His people and sees His son once again and says, "You are mine." The love of a perfect father accomplishes everything that sin never could.

Satisfaction.
> *Fulfillment.*
>> *Contentment.*
>>> *Wholeness.*
>>>> *Fullness.*
>>>>> *Joy.*
>>>>>> *Hope.*
>>>>>>> *Rest.*

The invitation to be with God was an invitation to know God, to know Him for who He is again, to know His character and nature—the loving goodness of a father. The psalmist writes, "Oh, taste and see that the Lord is good" (Psalm 34v8). Love seeks to repair and restore that which is broken and needy. Love moves toward the mess. It occupies the space between, refusing to allow the ugly to take root and grow. Love engages, rejecting passivity. Love gets involved. Love tills the hardened soil of our hearts until it's fertile to accept the seed. Then out of the new, good ground blossoms a bountiful garden. New life blooms from the fertile ground of love. This is the kind of love that God has for His people. In the Old Testament, this love was known as *hesed* love. Often translated "loving-kindness," *hesed* love is a stubborn love. It is described as a one-way love or a love-without-an-exit-strategy kind of love. It is a covenantal love that binds people together. It's this kind of love, a covenantal love, that makes God's people a covenantal people. This kind of love carries with it a sense of intimacy, a deep sense of knowing. Love longs to be known, so love pursues.

It's a covenant-making, commitment-keeping, grace-filled, I'm-not-going-anywhere, stubborn kind of love.

"Hesed is opposite of the spirit of our age, which says we have to act on our feelings. Hesed says, 'No, you act on your commitments. The feelings will follow." Love like this is unbalanced, uneven. There is nothing fair about this kind of love. But commitment-love lies at the heart of Christianity. It is Jesus's love for us at the cross, and it is to be our love for one another."
Paul Miller [3]

The New Testament picture of deep and intimate knowing displays beautiful imagery, as well. The second-most-used word for "know" in the NT is *ginosko*. It implies and presupposes a deep sense of personal knowing. Deep knowing happens with proximity and intimacy. There is an authentic and real personal experience that informs the knowing. It breeds understanding. It moves beyond simply knowing about a person or event from an outside source, several layers removed. It is firsthand information. It's an "I was there" kind of knowing. **We cannot simply rely on other people's experiences to move us**. With the amount of accessibility we now have, constantly and always connected, we run the risk of living our lives through other people's experiences. We become consumers over contributors. Restless, chaotic, searching for more. Constant and continual secondhand information at best can only manufacture and fabricate results. We risk becoming products in place of people. But *hesed* love breaks our hearts free. It pulls us out of the assembly line of society and pushes us into more. It keeps hope alive. It says, "I love you for you. I want you. You are mine. Be with me."

"...so that Christ may dwell in your hearts through faith—that you, being rooted and grounded in love, may have strength to comprehend with all the saints what is the

breadth and length and height and depth, and to know the love of Christ that sur-passes knowledge, that you may be filled with all the fullness of God."
Ephesians 3v17-19

The kind of love that God has for His people produces this kind of knowing. *Hesed* love plants *ginosko* knowing. Deeply personal, close in proximity, and abounding intimacy creates covenant-making, commitment-keeping, grace-filled, I'm-not-going-anywhere, stubborn kind of love. *Hesed* love invites humanity back into proximity and intimacy with creator God. *Hesed* love initiates the journey back home and makes the return possible. The journey is fueled by hope, and it's hope that keeps us moving. Hope in something more, invitation into something bigger. Belief that there is confidence in the risk. When hope roots in the fertile soil of love, it begins to create a deep sense of trust. What we learn to hope in, we will ultimately learn to trust. May trust move us back home. Home is where we experience intimacy and *knowing* begins.

I once heard someone say that humanity's greatest fear and greatest desire are intrinsically linked. At the core, what people really want is to be truly known and truly loved. Paradoxically, our greatest fear is that if we are truly known we cannot be truly loved. This phenomenon causes many of the relational problems that we experience today. We are becoming a mask-wearing world. We masquerade around, defined by soundbites, 140-characters utterances, and filtered Instagram pictures. Social media has given us innumerable tools to create masks that allow us to control how people know us. We've become professionals at managing the perception through which we want people to view us. **Since Adam and Eve attempted to cover their shame with fig leaves, humanity has been trying to cover its mass deficiencies by any and every means possible.** Our relationships are getting more and more superficial; all the while our hearts are longing to be loved. This is why grace is such a difficult thing for us to understand. Grace says that God's love is not earned or merited but rather given freely. Grace says you are loved despite who you are and in spite of your performance. Grace does not speak the language of reciprocity.

Learning to cultivate an environment of grace with our children is

WE CANNOT SIMPLY RELY ON OTHER
PEOPLE'S EXPERIENCE TO MOVE US.

incredibly difficult. Drew Dyck says, "The gospel is a difficult message because it is a message of humility in an age of arrogance." [4] Every other environment in which our children exist will be merit-based. Our children will have friends and lose friends based on behavior alone. They will get a specific mark in school, will be accepted into college, and will land jobs based on their performance. We live in a meritocracy. The entire world will be screaming, "Do better, do more, try harder;" all the while, Jesus whispers, "I am already enough, which means I love you no matter what." The home is the one place where grace can be lodged into the hearts of our children as they go out to engage the world. Our children initially learn about God's love in many ways through our love for them. I have to fight for grace in my home, which means my kids have to see me fail--and in the midst of my failures be loved and accepted by the Father. They have to see me let them fail and respond with grace. This type of grace says *your worth and value are intrinsic, your beauty and dignity come from the one who made you. As an image bearer of the creator, perfected through the work of Jesus, you are not lovable because you do good, but rather you are lovable because you are lovely. I am proud of you because you are my son. You are deeply loved because you are my daughter.* This is what our children need to learn if they are ever going to be free from the demands of a mask-wearing, performance-driven, cutthroat, pull-yourself-up-by-your-bootstraps kind of world.

Parents, it starts with us. Are you experiencing God's all-sufficient grace today? If not, then let's cry out to the Father in truth. Let's ask the Holy Spirit to lead us to a deeper belief of God's grace.

There a significant lack of knowing in our families, perhaps this lack of knowing is due to the void of experiencing *hesed* in our homes.

May our love be a tangible expression of the Father's love.

May our children bloom in the garden of grace.

READ

Ephesians 2v8-9, 4v20-24; John 1v16, 17v3, 3v16-17; 2 Corinthians 12v9; Romans 3v20-24, 5v8, 6v14, 11v6; Acts 15v11; 2 Peter 1v2; James 4v6; Numbers 6v25; Colossians 1v15-23

MEMORIZE

Jesus came to rescue us so that we could: know Him.
We can know Him because He gives us: grace.
He gives us grace even though we: don't deserve it.
We don't deserve it because of: our sin/rebellion.
Sin separates, but Jesus brings us back: home with God.

CHAT

Q: What is grace?
A: Free and unmerited favor; receiving what we do not deserve; salvation.

Q: What does it mean to know God? Do we deserve to know God?
A: Sin separates us because of our rebellion, but grace brings us back home to be with God. To know Jesus is to know the Father (Col. 1v15-23).

Q: When we receive grace, what do we experience?
A: Undeserved love, forgiveness, humility, peace. We experience the gospel.

Q: What did we learn about God?
A: He is generous, a bottomless ocean of grace, an endless vault of more.

Q: Where/how do we see the gospel?
A: We don't deserve to receive God's love, but He pursues and gives love freely.

PRAY

God, You created us to know You, to be with You and to take care of Your creation, but our sin disrupted and destroyed everything. Sin aligned our desires and our passions with our own selfishness. Forgive us for not trusting You and believing You. You generously pour out Your grace so that we can know You and be with You and so that we can learn how to take care of Your creation. Your love is extravagant and limitless; it knows no bounds. Your grace covers our shame and makes us new. Your love holds everything together. Amen.

JESUS CAME TO RESCUE US SO THAT WE COULD

KNOW HIM.

WE CAN KNOW HIM BECAUSE HE GIVES US

GRACE.

HE GIVES US GRACE EVEN THOUGH WE

DON'T DESERVE IT.

WE DON'T DESERVE IT BECAUSE OF

OUR SIN,
OUR REBELLION.

SIN SEPARATES, BUT JESUS BRINGS US BACK

HOME WITH GOD.

13
HOLINESS

For our sake He made Him to be sin who knew no sin, so that in Him we might become the righteousness of God.
2 Corinthians 5v21

As obedient children, do not be conformed to the passions of your former ignorance, but as he who called you is holy, you also be holy in all your conduct, since it is written, "You shall be holy, for I am holy."
1 Peter 1v14-16

Since the beginning, God has been revealing who He is on His terms. The revelation of His heart, through His character and nature, is called theology. It's who God says He is, as specifically revealed in the pages of the scriptures. These innumerable attributes of God, the depths of which we are unable to mine, and His inexhaustible majesty are nonetheless made available to us through the scriptures. Throughout history, humanity has exhausted language and diction in an effort to better articulate who God is and what He is like. Our best words and attempts still fall short to fully describe Him. He is other, more, beyond, yet He's here, near, and with His creation. He is infinitely good, and wholly just. He is completely and wholly self-sufficient and without need. He is righteous and good. He is other and set apart.

He is the image of the invisible God, the firstborn of all creation. For by him all things were created, in heaven and on earth, visible and invisible, whether thrones or dominions or rulers or authorities-all things were created through him and for him. And he is before all things, and in him all things hold together. And he is the head of the body, the church. He is the beginning, the firstborn from the dead, that in everything he might be preeminent. For in him all the fullness of God was pleased to dwell, and through him to reconcile to himself all things, whether on earth or in heaven, making peace by the blood of his cross.
Colossians 1v15-20

For it was indeed fitting that we should have such a high priest, holy, innocent, unstained, separated from sinners, and exalted above the heavens.
Hebrews 7v26

Jesus is holy. He is absolutely holy and set apart, which means that He is absolutely untainted, unblemished, flawless, full, and unlimited in all He does. This is a picture of purity. It denotes someone or something that is without defect. There is no way to improve it or make it better. It is already perfect. Jesus's holiness is the essential piece of His character that is necessary to be in the presence of a holy, perfect, just, and righteous father. Without holiness, we cannot be in proximity with the father, thus having no intimacy. Without the covering of righteousness, we cannot truly know God. Sin separates and creates distance. Sin drives us further from intimacy with God. This is the pursuit of the adversary and the great lie. To manipulate and distort truth that drives us further from true and right belief. Behind all of sin is unbelief. The distance exposes our unbelief. The longing unveils our sin. The separation reveals our deep desperation. It's proximity and closeness that the heart of humanity longs for. It was closeness and proximity... a *withness* that saturated Eden. The holiness and righteousness of God, the essential character and nature that created, was what humanity knew. It's what we were created out of and for. Distance and separation is what Jesus rescues us from, and holiness and intimate knowing is what Jesus saves us to. Through Him, by Him, to Him, for Him, Jesus saves. The perfection, righteousness, and holiness of Jesus were essential to cover our unbelief. God the father, full of mercy and grace, covers Adam's and Eve's nakedness in the garden with the skin of animals. Blood was shed to cover at the beginning, and it will be necessary to cover in the end.

As humanity continued to move further from the place it was created to be (the writer of Genesis calls this "east of Eden"), God never stopped loving His creation. Humanity's sin kept Adam and Eve from God's holiness, but He was never far. He made a promise, and His promise He would keep. God appointed priests who would advocate on behalf of the people to God, prophets who would advocate on behalf of God to His people, and kings who would be appointed to bring some sort of order to the chaos. God also instituted the sacrificial system in the Old Testament. This system was the means by which, through grace and mercy, God allowed His people to atone for their sins through the sacrifice of an animal. "Atonement" is satisfying someone or something for an offense committed. This system required the blood sacrifice of an unblemished, pure, and spotless lamb. The whole of the Old Testament, every book, pointed toward the great sacrifice that would be necessary to make the great rescue possible. The sacrificial offering—that Jesus would lay His life down for us, taking our sin that causes death and giving us His righteousness—that gives life. The writer of Hebrews refers to the Old Testament as a "shadow of things to come." Everything pointed to the cross and the shed blood of Jesus that atones for our sin and makes salvation possible.

Only the holiness of Jesus can cover our sin and reveal our unbelief. Only the perfect blood shed by Jesus can atone for our sin and invite us back home. The sacrificial atonement of Jesus freely, willingly, and obediently giving His life for us can bring us back into communion with the father. We must be presented holy to attend the presence of God. God not only covers our sin but also imputes or puts His righteousness on us. Just like the prodigal son who returns home, the faithful father clothes himtttg as his son and not as his servant. "But the father said to his servants, 'Bring quickly the best robe, and *put it on him*, and put a ring on his hand, and shoes on his feet" (Luke 15v22). It's the same phrase the apostle Paul uses in his letter to the Ephesians, " to put on the new self, created after the likeness of God in true righteousness and holiness" (Ephesians 4v24). In Paul's letter to the church in Corinth, he writes, "Therefore, if anyone is in Christ, he is a new creation. The old has passed away; behold, the new has come" (2 Corinthians 5v17). The great sacrifice of Jesus is the means of new creation, restoration, and newness. His righteousness gives us new life and assures our invitation home to be with Him. His holiness is the source of our confidence as we walk in the here-and-now and await the yet-to-come.

...so that he might present the church to himself in splendor, without spot or wrinkle or any such thing, that she might be holy and without blemish.
Ephesians 5v27

And you, who once were alienated and hostile in mind, doing evil deeds, he has now reconciled in his body of flesh by his death, in order to present you holy and blameless and above reproach before him.
Colossians 1v21-22

The great lie promised a complete life of peace apart from God. The adversary sought to manipulate a life away from its primal source. As we experience longing and separation, the repercussions of the fall remind us there is more. As the adversary continues to weave his story and seduce the beloved away, the father reminds us that to be with Him is better. Only holiness can cover and create belonging.

How are we experiencing the holiness of God in our families?

The old has passed away; behold, the new has come.
2 Corinthians 5v17

I (David) repeat that verse to myself often. As humans, we have a tendency to equate familiarity with comfort, even if it is harmful. This is why people often go back to their old patterns of destructive behavior. As a pastor, I have counseled many people who continually go back to patterns of destructive behavior, and when we get to the heart of the issue, the refrain I experience most often is, "This is all I know." As parents, we are not exempt from this reality. Learning about the newness and otherness of God is important to our understanding of the invitation we have received from Him. We are invited to participate in something new and different, something other than what the world has to offer. As exciting as this invitation sounds for most of us, this can be incredibly scary. I am not sure what lies on the other side of my obedience, but I know exactly what lies on the other side of my disobedience. I have been there. "As a dog returning to his own vomit, so fools repeat their folly" (Proverbs 26:11). As horrible as that sounds, all of us can relate. We tend to find comfort in what we know and what we have experienced. We frequent the same restaurants and order the same meals, reluctant to navigate something untried. We tend to think we are adventurous, but something new and untested cannot be calculated fully. There is a real level of risk required to step out into those waters. Changing our parenting styles and natural go-to responses are not easy. They are not familiar. I have to remind myself that God is doing something new. In Isaiah 55v8, God reminds us of an important truth. He says, "My thoughts are not your thoughts, neither are your ways my ways." God is other, He is different, and in many ways we do not understand because our earthly experience is so incomparably constrained, so limited. But

WE TEND TO THINK WE ARE
ADVENTUROUS, BUT SOMETHING
NEW AND UNTESTED CANNOT BE
CALCULATED FULLY. THERE IS A REAL
LEVEL OF RISK REQUIRED TO STEP OUT
INTO THOSE WATERS.

here is what I know: God is good. With His goodness comes the invitation to participate in something new. We know that in God, there is life. We know that in God, there is freedom. We know that in God, there is redemption and safety. The more we follow Him, on His terms, in His ways, and in His design, the more we will find comfort in obedience. The same is true for our children.

May our children come to know the all-sufficiency of Christ.

READ

2 Corinthians 5v21; Hebrews 7v26; 1 Peter 1v19; Ephesians 1v4; Colossians 1v12-18; Psalms 29v2, 33v21, 47v8, 96v9, 103v1, 105v3, 145v7; Isaiah 6v3, 40v21-31, 43v15, 57v15; Deuteronomy 32v4; 1 Samuel 2v2

MEMORIZE

We are all broken and full of sin, but: Jesus has never sinned.
He has never sinned because: He is holy.
To be holy means: to be set apart.
To be set apart means: to be like God.
To be like God means: to be righteous and perfect.

CHAT

Q: What is sin? What does our sin remind us of?
A: Any time we don't trust in and believe God. Our neediness and desperation for God.

Q: Can we trust God? Why?
A: Yes. He has never sinned. He is holy and perfect. He loves us. Jesus is God, and God has never sinned. We have need that can only be met by Jesus.

Q: What is worship?
A: To worship means to ascribe worth. Jesus is worthy of our trust and belief and full attention.

Q: What did we learn about God?
A: He is holy, set apart, unlike anything or anyone else. He is righteous and perfect.

Q: Where/how do we see the gospel?
A: God is set apart, but He came to us out of His holiness and love. He pursues us to be with Him.

PRAY

God, the temptation to go my own way is always before me, because my sin distorts my desires and entices my passions away from You. My sin keeps me from You, but Your love and Your grace invite me and welcome me to be at home with You. You alone are holy, unlike everything and everyone else; You alone are righteous, the ultimate standard we live by. You alone are perfect, always in obedience to Your father. Your perfect love holds everything together. Amen.

WE ARE ALL BROKEN AND FULL OF SIN, BUT
JESUS HAS NEVER SINNED.

HE HAS NEVER SINNED BECAUSE

HE IS HOLY.

TO BE HOLY MEANS
TO BE SET APART.

TO BE SET APART MEANS
TO BE LIKE GOD.

TO BE LIKE GOD MEANS
TO BE RIGHTEOUS AND PERFECT.

14
JESUS IS BETTER

The LORD appeared to him from far away. "I have loved you with an everlasting love; therefore I have continued my faithfulness to you."
Jeremiah 31v3

Beat down by the constant barrage of the enemy, our souls can only find rest in Jesus. The longing exposes the continual search for rest; the pasture beside still waters with God is the only place our souls know refuge. This pasture is home with our good shepherd. What we hope in, we learn to trust. What we trust, we will depend on.

Humanity has always been in search of wide open spaces. The unexplored frontiers, full of mystery and intrigue. No boundaries, undomesticated, untamed, and wild, the allure is vibrantly within us. Call it wanderlust, call it adventure, maybe even call it liberty; freedom has always been close to the heart of humanity.

What is it in us that longs for the open road?

What is it that drives us to new frontiers?

What if our desire for wide open spaces is really a deep desire for rest?

What if the invitation to rest is the invitation into the land of freedom?

What if freedom isn't what we always thought it was?

The Spirit of the Lord is upon me, because he has anointed me to proclaim good news to the poor. He has sent me to proclaim liberty to the captives and recovering of sight to the blind, to set at liberty those who are oppressed...
Luke 4v18

Perhaps the great mystery of freedom is dependence. Freedom isn't the void of need but rather the dependence upon the One who can actually fulfill our deepest need. Freedom isn't the absence of boundaries but rather clear and defined invitation—our souls refreshed and restored in a place of security, relief, and provision in the presence of the good shepherd.

Biblical writers use the metaphor of sheep to illustrate us, the church, the people of God. These animals are a bit mindless, completely defenseless, incredibly dependent, and needy. They easily tend to wander off and get lost. Anxious, sheep find it difficult to rest.

Does this resonate?

"The LORD is my shepherd; I shall not want. He makes me lie down in green pastures. He leads me beside still waters. He restores my soul."
Psalm 23v1-3

The biblical concept of rest is beautifully deep and profound. In the Old Testament, God refers to Himself as the good shepherd, a phrase Jesus will speak of himself. The psalmist writes, He, the good shepherd, "leads me beside still or quiet waters and restores my soul." This word *still* or *quiet*, is the same word from which we get rest. It's the idea of settled security, where peace, quiet, and trust are present. It conveys the idea of relief. It's in this place, with Him, that our souls are restored. It's a place of belonging. As defenseless and anxious sheep, under the care, protection, and provision of our shepherd, we will find rest, security and strength again. Jesus echoes this invitation, "Come to me and you will find rest" (Matthew 11v28). The word *restores* used by King David in Psalm 23v3 connotes this meaning of "turn" or "return." It carries with it the idea of repentance. It's the idea of a turning away from and turning toward. We hear the good shepherd say, "Come to me."

"Repentance often drives the journey of love. It moves the story forward."
Paul Miller [5]

The apostle Paul claims that the love of Jesus is compelling (2 Cor. 5v14) and controlling. It woos us and pursues us. The *hesed* love of God sends His son Jesus to the cross, and Jesus, full of *hesed* love, resolutely finishes, fulfills, and satisfies. His love is fierce. Jesus makes the bold, offensive, and provocative claim against the cultural expectation and the eminent accusations, "...I am the way, and the truth, and the life. No one comes to the Father except through me" (John 14v6). His proposal to go to Him takes us beyond just mere conviction. Repentance requires a return.

The invitation to rest is the invitation to return.

Turn away from and turn toward.

Return is the invitation to freedom.

"You have made us for yourself, O Lord, and our heart is restless until it rests in you."
St. Augustine [6]

We are offered freedom, invitation to experience rest. Freedom from trying to merit and earn our place of belonging. Freedom from trying to prove our worth and significance. Freedom from trying to make our own way in the world. Freedom from having to control and manipulate to better serve our selfish agendas. Freedom to rest in the finished work of Jesus on the cross, which has completely and sufficiently satisfied every righteous demand of God.

For freedom Christ has set us free; stand firm therefore, and do not submit again to a yoke of slavery.
Galatians 5v1

He restores my soul.
Psalm 23v3

The great rescue is the means of reconciliation. It's the way back home. Jesus is the better Eden. The life, death, and resurrection of Jesus awaken the *imago dei* within humanity; they restore our invitation to join Him and steward the call to represent Him. By His righteousness we are healed. Through faith alone, by grace alone, from God alone, the garden longings deep within humanity are being satisfied. Our identity resurfaces. Shalom returns.

Once again, we know who we are.

The invitation goes forth again... Join me.

We exist for no greater purpose than to glorify God by pointing to the fullness of His glorious provision in Christ! It is in Him only that we finally find shalom. Jesus is better. He is the answer. He is life. Teaching our children to look there first is the task that lies before us as parents. We were born into the belief that we are the center of all that exists. For so many years, we believed that the earth was the center of our solar system. I think the same thing is true for us individually. We live as if we are the center of all that is important, which is why the paltry and petty taste for the lesser things of this world overpower the eternal taste for the things of God. If we become the center, then we can only offer what we have: broken, insufficient, powerless, and agenda-filled effort. We operate out of our utter deficiency in place of Christ's fullness (Ephesians 1v3). It is an impossible task and causes a constant state of exhaustion and frustration. The more we begin to see Christ as the center of all that exists, the more we look to Him for meaning and purpose. The more we look to Him for meaning and purpose, the more we will find it. In Him there is life. Where we find Him, we will find rest. Right now, as a family, we are helping our children to look up. The concept is that we spend so much time trying to satisfy our own desires that we rarely look up to see the way that Jesus is at work, the way he alone is quenching and satisfying our thirst. I am reminded of Jesus's interaction with the woman at the well. Jesus says, "If you knew the gift of God, and who it is that is saying to you, 'Give me a drink,' you would have asked him, and he would have given you living water" (John 4v10). The woman was so consumed with herself that she missed the source of everything she desired. Yes, she was filled with shame, but she only saw herself. We walk this earth with our eyes fixed on ourselves and we miss the center; we miss the life; we miss Christ. Jesus is better! Helping our children to look up just might lead them to fixing their eyes on Christ. Think about how most suburban American parents relate to their children: soccer, ballet, guitar lessons. Everything is always about them and has them at the center. I am not saying those things are bad. Those things can be amazing! But if we do not learn how to teach our kids the value of others and the value of sacrifice, then they will have a hard time spotting Christ.

May our children come to find that they exist for a greater purpose beyond themselves.

READ

John 1v29 & 36, 3v16, 15v12-13, 20; 1 John 1v9, 4v8-19; Philippians 2v9-11; Hebrews 1v3; Isaiah 53v6; Psalms 103v12, 51v7, 32v2; 1 Peter 1v18-19; Ephesians 1v7-8; 2v13; Romans 1v5; 3v25; 4v7; 5v11; Colossians 1v12-14

MEMORIZE

Jesus had to be holy, righteous, and perfect in order to: rescue us.
Jesus' perfection: covers our sin.
He rescued us by: dying on a cross.
But three days later: He rose from the grave.
He came back to life because: God's love is bigger and better than sin.

CHAT

Q: Why is it important to know that Jesus is holy?
A: Holiness is what makes Him God, set apart from us, perfect in every way, able to rescue us and cover our sin.

Q: What time of the year do we remember and celebrate Jesus' life over death?
A: Easter. What does Easter represent? Jesus is better and bigger than sin. (See: EASTER catechism) EXPERIENCE: observe communion as a family (see additional resources).

Q: Was the cross necessary?
A: Yes. To cover our sin, to take our place, so we could live with Him and enjoy Him—all for His glory.

Q: What did we learn about God?
A: He is powerful; He is gracious. He sent His son for me, for His glory.

Q: Where/how do we see the gospel?
A: Jesus didn't deserve to die. In obedience, He went to the cross for me.

PRAY

God, You sent Your one and only holy, righteous, and perfect son Jesus into the brokenness and pain of the world. You sent Him to show the world who You are and what love looks like. You gave up Your life for us so that we could have new life in You and live for You. Your love is bigger and better than our rebellion. Your grace is more satisfying and fulfilling than our sin. Your death defeated death. Your love holds everything together. Amen.

JESUS HAD TO BE HOLY, RIGHTEOUS, AND PERFECT IN ORDER TO

RESCUE US.

JESUS' PERFECTION

COVERS OUR SIN.

HE RESCUED US BY

DYING ON A

CROSS.

BUT THREE DAYS LATER

HE ROSE FROM THE GRAVE.

HE CAME BACK TO LIFE BECAUSE

GOD'S LOVE

IS BIGGER AND BETTER THAN SIN.

15
BELONGING

Come to me, all who labor and are heavy laden, and I will give you rest. Take my yoke upon you, and learn from me, for I am gentle and lowly in heart, and you will find rest for your souls. For my yoke is easy, and my burden is light.
Matthew 11v28-30

The invitation to be with God is an invitation to know God. The invitation to know God is the invitation to find rest in Him and belonging with Him. You are mine. Now be with me. The *withness* that saturated Eden is available now through the great rescue of Jesus.

The biblical narrative is full of intense and beautiful imagery from Eden to the cross. The imagery depicts a stubborn, one-way love *(hesed)* that never lets go, always pulling us back and beckoning a return. A first-hand experience, an intimate knowing and understanding *(ginosko)* that helps us navigate our way through the world. All the imagery, all the invitation, all to remind us. All to wake us from our slumber and revive our identity.

We are living in unprecedented times. We are always on, always connected. Emails, texts, social media alerts, breaking news, unfinished projects looming in an already crushing and over-committed lifestyle. Advertisements everywhere we look, competing for our attention, seeking to arrest our hearts and minds. What wasn't even a thought now becomes a desire. That desire becomes a purchase. More desires, more purchases, more debt. And for what? Constant temptation to keep up with the "whoevers" most often runs our families dry and were left wondering aimless.

School demands more of our children at a younger age, showing statistics that compare not to the school on the other side of town or even the other side of the country, but to the school on the other side of the world. The competition is always growing and is ever expanding. We are no longer competing for jobs with the people in our cities. The playing field is now worldwide. We are thrust into the mindset that makes our children move from a childhood of freedom to an upbringing of performance. Travel club sports teams are taking the place of everyday common recreational events. Brands are entering into new categories and targeting younger generations. Our children are growing up in a world that celebrates the skin-deep beautiful and marginalizes the ordinary. In a world built by consumerism, we are bombarded with facades and veneers. Drive this... wear this... live here... eat this, don't eat that... and you will be fulfilled. Restless and chaotic, full of anxiety, we've lost our way. This new narrative sets its roots deeper.

Sound familiar?

Remember the new storyline the adversary began to weave in the garden with Eve? The cunning tactic of distorted truth. "Eve, God is holding out on you, there's still more. He's holding the *more* back from you. You don't need Him anymore. You can be in control now." The great lie was targeted directly at her identity. It sought to arrest her heart and mind. The intent was to deceive her and manipulate her into thinking that the transcendent *more* was somewhere "out there," and that the only way to find it was to seek after it, to lust for it. The illusion was that after humanity hit the road in search of more, it would be enticed away from the way of the heart and remain on the surface. We fool around with finite things, chasing after the mirage of satisfaction, but they only propel us to keep consuming more.

The tactic and manipulation has created a world where performance is everything. What's in? Who's in? How do I get in? And then once I've earned my way in, how do I stay in? It's a world full of anxiety, restlessness, and chaos. Where will our souls go to find rest? Where will we go to find refuge? Where do we belong?

We must return home.
Back into the loving arms of our father.

Jesus's claim on the cross was, "It is finished" (John 19v30), perhaps the three greatest words ever uttered. Leonard Ravenhill said, "In these three words I see the consummation of all the Old Testament truth and the germination of all New Testament truth." [7] It is the perfect and complete finished work of Jesus on the cross that authoritatively makes return possible. These three words now mark every believer and beloved of Jesus.

The holy temple in Jerusalem was the center of Jewish religious activity. Worship according to the Law of Moses was carried out in the temple. In the back center of the temple lay the place of deepest significance for the Jews. It was called the Holy of Holies, and it was the earthly dwelling place of God's holiness, separated from the rest of the temple by a thick veil. The book of Exodus says the veil was fashioned from blue, purple, and scarlet material and fine-twisted linen, material that signified royalty and majesty. Only the high priest was permitted to pass through the veil into this place once a year on the Day of Atonement, to enter into God's presence for all of Israel and make atonement for their sins.

The scriptures state that the moment Jesus uttered the words, "*it is finished*" and took his last breath on the cross, the veil that separated the place of God's presence was torn in two from the top down. The veil symbolized Christ Himself as the only means possible to the father. This dramatic event symbolized that Jesus's death on the cross was a complete and sufficient atonement for the sins of humanity. The way into the Holy of Holies was opened to all, both Jew and Gentile. The cross established a new covenant made in blood and fulfilled perfectly everything that was necessary to be with God again. This is called reconciliation. For those who receive the invitation to submit to the sovereign king Jesus, there is no more enmity caused by sin between humanity and a holy God.

> *"When the veil hid us from you, your love broke through.*
> *Now we stand in your presence, found in you."*
> **Logan Miller** [8]

By the precious blood of Jesus spilt and the veil torn, God says, "You belong."

"Rest your weary heart here with me."

Receive the invitation, "Come, rest with me."

One of my (David) favorite stories about my son Moses happened when he had just turned three-years-old. My son loves to cuddle with daddy. After a long day, he was lying with me with his head on my stomach. He breathed deeply, and then I breathed deeply. The cadence of our hearts and breath were in sync and in that moment, for that specific space of time, there was an overwhelming sense that everything was perfect. And with an endearing look, my son looked up into my eyes, patted me on the belly, and said "I love my big fat daddy." As unflattering (and maybe a little true) as that statement was, I knew exactly what he meant.

He was home.

He was safe.

It was in the "bigness" of his father that he felt secure. In that moment, he knew he belonged. Although I am still trying to lose weight because of that moment, I am also trying to hang on to that image. God's design for His creation is that we would find safety underneath the shadow of His presence. One picture the Old Testament writers and poets often used was this image of protection. "Keep me as the apple of your eye; hide me in the shadow of your wings" (Psalm 17v8). This image gives the idea that our self-sufficiency would be replaced with being at home in the light of His all-sufficient presence. I desperately want my children to feel safe at home. But more than that, I want them to find their home and their belonging in the presence of God. He is their true and perfect Father, and as parents, we get to participate in the work of His love. It is an arduous journey filled with desperation. It is the life-giving work of setting up our homes in God the Father, through the sacrifice of the Son, by the power of the Spirit.

It is only there that we will truly belong.

It is where our families go to rest.

May our children come to see, and know, and experience the "bigness" of Jesus and may we find rest in His finished work.

READ

Matthew 11v28-30; John 17v3-5; Psalm 23v1-5; Colossians 1v21-22; Luke 15v11-32; Matthew 27v45-51; 2 Corinthians 5v17-21; Isaiah 40v28-31; 1 John 4v7-12; 1 John 4v17-19; Romans 5v1-2; Psalm 103v1-4

MEMORIZE

Remember, it is God's desire that man and woman would always: be with Him.
So Jesus never stops: pursuing.
Jesus puts the broken pieces: back together.
And offers us: rest and belonging.
Jesus is the way: back home.

CHAT

Q: What dos it mean to be with God? What does it mean to not be with God?
A: To be with God means to belong. Sin separates but the gospel creates belonging and brings us close.

Q: How did / does Jesus pursue?
A: The incarnation; (Christmas story: see Advent catechism) Jesus came to be with so we can be with Him.
In our unbelief, the work of the Holy Spirit convicts us of our sin, calls us to repentance, to receive grace.

Q: What does rest look like?
A: We don't have to perform to earn our worth. Jesus has accomplished everything that was and is necessary on our behalf. Invitation to be with God is the invitation to trust and believe in the finished work of Jesus.

Q: What did we learn about God?
A: God pursues us. He is gracious. He sent His son for me and for His glory.

Q: Where/how do we see the gospel?
A: The gospel creates belonging, and brings us back home. God loved us first. On our own, we cannot return.

PRAY

God, Your love is extravagant. Thank you for your never ending pursuit of our hearts. As the good shepherd, You lead us into spaces of quiet so that we may find complete rest. When we lie down, we are comforted by your promises. God you are our place of home and you richly provide everything with much grace. Thank you for the deep love and approval that we find only in You. We do not have to perform or run tirelessly to find who we are. May we rest in your nearness. Your love holds everything together. Amen.

EMEMBER, IT IS GOD'S DESIRE THAT MAN AND WOMAN WOULD ALWAYS

BE WITH HIM.

SO JESUS NEVER STOPS

PURSUING.

JESUS PUTS THE BROKEN PIECES

BACK TOGETHER.

AND OFFERS US

REST AND BELONGING.

JESUS IS THE WAY

BACK HOME.

RECREATION

MULTIPLY
THE SENT ONES
THE CHURCH
EVERYDAY LOVE
RETURN

Revelation 21v1-4
Then I saw a new heaven and a new earth, for the first heaven and the first earth had passed away, and the sea was no more. And I saw the holy city, new Jerusalem, coming down out of heaven from God, prepared as a bride adorned for her husband. And I heard a loud voice from the throne saying, "Behold, the dwelling place of God is with man. He will dwell with them, and they will be his people, and God himself will be with them as their God. He will wipe away every tear from their eyes, and death shall be no more, neither shall there be mourning, nor crying, nor pain anymore, for the former things have passed away."

1 Peter 5v10-11
And the God of all grace, who called you to his eternal glory in Christ, after you have suffered a little while, will himself restore you and make you strong, firm and steadfast. To him be the power for ever and ever. Amen.

THE GOSPEL IS THE TRUTH THAT JESUS ENTERED INTO THE HUMAN CONDITION TO RENEW, REBUILD, AND RESTORE ALL THINGS TO HIMSELF.

Jesus resolutely set out toward Jerusalem. He set his gaze to the cross and never looked back. Through anguish and pain, torment and public humiliation, in the face of mockery and abandonment, Jesus pilgrimaged to the cross to die the death that we deserved to die so that we could live the life we were created to live. God promised to be the perfect shepherd His people need most. He promised He would never leave or forsake His children. He knew this was the only way to fulfill the covenant He made with His people. God could only perfectly fulfill and satisfy His righteous standard of holiness and perfection. The substitutionary atonement of Jesus in our place, taking our shame and rebellion while simultaneously clothing us in His righteousness, is the only way humanity can know and be with the father again.

The scriptures say that with His last breath, Jesus said, "It is finished." Just like in Eden, the creator God breathed His breath and His spirit into the dust, and life burst forth. On the cross, Jesus breathed His last breath, perfectly fulfilled the covenant and satisfied the righteous demands of His father.

The breath of life breathed into humanity again!

This is good news!

God is a promise maker and a promise keeper. He alone always does what is good, right, and perfect. In accordance with the scriptures, Jesus had promised that three days later He would rise from the grave. In one fell swoop, the provocative claims and self-definitions of Jesus rang true. "I am the bread of life; I am the light of the world; I am the gate; I am the good shepherd; I am the resurrection and the life; I am the way, the truth, and the life; I am the vine."

"I love you."

"Come to me."

The gospel is the truth that Jesus entered into the human condition to renew, rebuild, and restore all things to Himself. The truth that creator God would literally and physically enter the depravity of the human experience and begin to put things back into their right and proper place through the work of His son Jesus. The gospel is Jesus getting involved with us. The gospel is the good news that Jesus is changing everything and making all things new. The gospel is the fullness of Jesus and how He fills everything in every way, and how His love holds everything together.

RECREATION catechism traces five main parts of God's motive behind creating: **MULTIPLY, THE SENT ONES, THE CHURCH, EVERYDAY LOVE, and RETURN.**

16
MULTIPLY

Jesus had been brutally murdered by the religious elite. Afraid of an insurrection and a dilution of their law, the religious leaders attempted to rid their community of Jesus and His teachings. They knew His movement was small, but the threat of growth was imminent. They bet on the fear tactic of Roman crucifixion and public humiliation to stunt the newly born Jesus Way. However, even the Roman governor, Pontius Pilate, could find no fault Jesus. In an effort to wash his hands clean of the proceedings, and to appease Jewish requests, perhaps maybe even to mitigate the growing unrest of the Jewish people, he caved to the mob and ordered Jesus to be crucified. Led by the chief priest Caiaphas, the alleged offense was blasphemy. Jesus claimed to be the Son of God, Messiah, the promised One for whom Israel had been waiting. The religious leaders had been tasked with keeping Israel pure and prepared for the arrival of messiah. Jesus, the long-awaited promised rescuer, arrived. He came, lived among them, preached the coming kingdom of God, and made a new way forward...

But they missed Him.
> *Then they killed Him.*

The religious leaders believed there was no way the rumors of resurrection were possible. This idealistic pagan talk seemed more rooted in mystical fairytale than historic truth passed down from their forefathers. If they killed the leader, then they killed the heartbeat of the movement.

Jesus's followers were stunned and confused. For three years, they had followed Him closely—daily—and witnessed miracle after miracle which no words could describe. Jesus taught them about the kingdom of God and what it meant to be with Him, how to live together, and how to love one another. His teachings were revolutionary and powerful. He taught like none of their other teachers had ever taught. They were amazed by His words. Now, in the immediate wake of the death of their rabbi, they were lost and devastated.

Some fled, others hid, and one by the name of Peter even denied he knew Jesus at all. They all wondered what the last three years had been for. The Jesus Way appeared to be over. They had little faith that He would actually rise from the tomb behind the stoned entrance.

With the future of His movement hanging in the balance, the disciples of Jesus were forced to wrestle with their unbelief. If there is no resurrection, there is no movement; no Jesus, *no Jesus Way*. Everything was centered on His faithfulness.

Either He is or He isn't.

Either He is everything, or He is nothing.

The faithless disciples losing heart in their faithful leader still lurks in us now. Is He really who He says He is? Will He really do what He promised He would do? Jesus has always been trustworthy and constant, always faithful and never-failing. He said three days. These would be a tumultuous and difficult three days. Embracing the momentary ambiguity and the profound paradox of death giving way to life was up to them. Resurrection was up to God.

Cynicism is one of the mightiest religions of our day. Cynicism finds the status quo and sets up camp. The reality is that we've got much to be cynical about. The constant pain of the human experience leaves us wanting. Repeated empty promises of more get stuck in the mundane. The voice of the cynic says, "This is as good as it gets. No sense in hoping and trusting; they'll just let you down; they always do." Pain sets in, loneliness follows, and we run the risk of getting lost in our suffering. Sucked into a world we think no one else understands, it seems impossible to remember the goodness of God and scandalous grace of Jesus when the pain is so acute, when pain is so present. The pilgrimage of trust and truth is forged through the path of pain. Like childbirth, there is no new life without pain, and new life was coming through Jesus. The hint of hope forges a tiny resurrection in our hearts. The disciples waited; they hoped.

Resurrection was in the air.

The promise maker kept His promise... He always does.

Despite death's deepest desires and its darkest days, death was defeated and the grave was overcome.

The Jesus Way was not over. In fact, it had just begun.

Jesus, victorious over death and the triumphant over the grave, galvanized the messianic promises and cemented His message. Jesus defeated sin and death and displayed His supremacy as sovereign king over all.

He is the image of the invisible God, the firstborn of all creation. For by him all things were created, in heaven and on earth, visible and invisible, whether thrones or dominions or rulers or authorities-all things were created through him and for him. And he is before all things, and in him all things hold together. And he is the head of the body, the church. He is the beginning, the firstborn from the dead, that in everything he might be preeminent. For in him all the fullness of God was pleased to dwell, and through him to reconcile to himself all things, whether on earth or in heaven, making peace by the blood of his cross.
Colossians 1v15-20

The truth is that the story of God has always moved toward resurrection. The sweeping narrative of the master storyteller was always intended to journey into new life. God promised His chosen people that He would make them a great nation and that they would be blessed in order to bless the world. The covenant God made Abraham in Genesis 12 has been completely and fully fulfilled through Jesus's finished work on the cross. He keeps His promises. He established this new covenant through His sacrificial and substitutionary death and His triumphant victory over the grave. This single act of love accomplished everything that was necessary to satisfy the penalty of sin. The people of God, marked by the atoning blood of Jesus, would again join God in His work.

The commission is the work of renewal.

Over the course of the next forty days, the resurrected Jesus continued to show Himself to His disciples, and their faith increased as He continued to teach them more about the kingdom of God. The established kingdom of God was unlike any kingdom they had ever heard of or experienced. Instead of hatred and brutality, the kingdom of God is a people of love, grace, and truth. In place of conquering through armies of force, the kingdom of God moves on the rhythms of grace and conquers with truth and love. This new life in hope conquers deep-rooted cynicism while God renews His creation and reestablishes Edenic intentions.

God greatly multiplied the number of disciples after the resurrection. The message of Jesus went further than the disciples had ever imagined. The first followers of Jesus were called disciples. A disciple is a student, a learner who follows his teacher and becomes like his teacher. Disciples begin to sound like their teachers and look like them, act like them and talk like them. But disciples of Jesus are more than just mere pupils or students; Jesus calls them family: brothers and sisters, sons and daughters of the living God. As God's chosen people, set apart and distinct, blessed to be a blessing, the family of God tangibly represents who and what God is like.

But to all who did receive him, who believed in his name, he gave the right to become children of God, who were born, not of blood nor of the will of the flesh nor of the will of man, but of God.
John 1v12-13

A new commandment I give to you, that you love one another: just as I have loved you, you also are to love one another. By this all people will know that you are my disciples,if you have love for one another."
John 13v34-35

Resurrection made multiplication possible. There is no movement without resurrection. No Jesus Way. But the resurrection of Jesus invites deeper belief. It further establishes the trustworthiness of His message and cements His supreme kingly place over creation. It beckons a return; here and now, it satisfies the garden longings of our souls and invites us back to be with Him again.

Living in light of Jesus' resurrection as a parent is a lot easier said than done. On paper it is a wonderful ideology; in everyday life it is a constant battle. Jesus' invitation to us is rest and eternal life, but everyday life can feel like a burden and a kind of slow death (especially if you have children six and under). Where is that John 10v10 life we were promised? Where is the full, abundant life of eternal discovery?

When God saved me (David) and my wife Tara, we had these lofty visions of victorious and God-honoring lives, ready to charge hell with water pistols. We always made plans and had dreams that never included roadblocks, failure, and heartache. Funny how that works! Our hearts longed to do great things in the name of Jesus; we were ready to take on anything the Lord brought our way! Then God gave us children -- everything changed. How is it these sweet, little, bundles of joy can so quickly suck the life out of you while simultaneously giving a giant picture of true, genuine, covenantal love? *As we have been on this journey of parenting, trying to find our stride as a family, one thing we've learned over and over again is that idealism and comparison will rob us of the present joy that awaits in the everyday stuff of life.* The resurrection of Christ means that we do not have to compare, and we do not have to prove ourselves to the world. Our identity as parents is no longer wrapped up in our children's behavior but now we are free to trust in the power of Christ's life, death, and resurrection. Christ's resurrection means that we no longer have to pretend we are something we are not. It also means we do not have to perform to maintain a certain image. We can see both our failure and success in parenting as opportunities to find joy and trust in the Lord. Trusting in Christ's resurrection is where we find rest and hope in the midst of the struggle. We experience the work of Christ in the everyday moments of life. Moments when one of our children throws a fit at the grocery store or embarrasses us in front of our friends with their rebellious attitude. We experience the life of Christ when our first response is no longer anger and shame but rather a genuine longing for their little hearts to know the God who rescues us.

May we learn to trust more deeply in the work of Jesus and may we find deep confidence in the power of Christ's resurrection.

READ

John 3v16-17, 5v24; Isaiah 40v21-31; Matthew 28v18-20; 1 John 4v7-12; 1 Corinthians 9v22; Romans 1v16; Acts 1v8, 8v4-25; Luke 19v10; 2 Timothy 2v15; Psalm 73v28

MEMORIZE

God wanted the whole world: to know Him.
And to know: His love.
The first people who knew Jesus were called: His disciples.
The disciples: followed Jesus everywhere.
After the resurrection, God would greatly multiply: the number of disciples.

CHAT

Q: What does it mean to know God?
A: To know God is to know love, experience grace, and receive forgiveness of our sins.

Q: What is a disciple?
A: Student, yes, but more than a student... Jesus considered His disciples family. God humbled Himself in Jesus to share in the everyday rhythms of life with everyday people.

Q: What do you think it means to follow Jesus and His ways?
A: Picture of obedience; to live in freedom; to learn the ways of love; access in invitation.

Q: What did we learn about God?
A: His love is big; He is an inviting God; He gives access to Himself; He desires to be with us.

Q: Where/how do we see the gospel?
A: Jesus is God with us; we see/know God through Jesus.

PRAY

God, Your love is big enough for the entire world to see, to feel, to know, and to trust. Covering every person, every skin color, every language, every man and woman... Your love is full and vast. Like the master artist who created everything in the beginning of the story, Your creativity and imagination are put on display in the diversity of humanity. Each one of us represents a piece of You, and as we follow You, You put Your glory on display for us to see. Your love is big enough to hold everything together. Amen.

GOD WANTED THE WHOLE WORLD
TO KNOW HIM.
AND TO KNOW
HIS LOVE.

THE FIRST PEOPLE WHO KNEW JESUS WERE CALLED
HIS DISCIPLES.

THE DISCIPLES
FOLLOWED JESUS
EVERYWHERE.

AFTER THE RESURRECTION, GOD WOULD GREATLY MULTIPLY
THE NUMBER OF DISCIPLES.

17
THE SENT ONES

They tried to kill Jesus and destroy His movement, but the resurrection only multiplied His message. There was a new way forward now, a new way to live, a new way to be human. This new way looked like Jesus and loved like Jesus. The new rhythms of grace, peace, truth, and love displayed the heart of the king. This movement was known as the *Jesus Way* in the earliest days. Its message was brimming with new life and was full of good news. The good news is that there is now a new way. This good news is the gospel of Jesus Christ.

Jesus had been alluding to a time when He would no longer physically be present with His followers. As a master teacher and master disciple-maker, Jesus had been preparing His students for this time. Throughout their nearly three years of training with Jesus, there had been multiple times where Jesus had given His disciples authority to preach and teach and heal. He had sent them out in pairs to go together and tell their villages and communities of what they had experienced about the kingdom of God (Matthew 10). Jesus knew the task would be difficult and intimidating. He warned them of certain persecution and opposition; "You will be whipped and beaten and jailed for your allegiance to me. You will be taken to the authorities and held accountable for your actions." In the throes of anxiety and overwhelming realities of following their rabbi, Jesus brings peace and confidence. He tells them, "But do not be afraid." Three times, Jesus assures them and reassures them of His provision. The cost of being a disciple of Jesus is coming into clarity. Obedience was taking on a new life.

Surely the disciples of Jesus remembered these stories and these teachings. They remembered the excursions on which Jesus sent them into the villages to preach and teach; the difficulties they experienced whilst sent out in obedience; the times some received them and their message and the times people rejected them and refused to listen; the way the faithful father perfectly provided everything they needed as they watched His name move in their communities. Perhaps all of this was to prepare them for Jesus's final words, his final teaching, his grandest invitation and most profound command. Jesus's final words to his disciples before He returned to eternal glory with His father are powerful words engraved onto the hearts on every believer of Jesus. These words are known as the Great Commission.

And Jesus came and said to them, "All authority in heaven and on earth has been given to me. Go therefore and make disciples of all nations, baptizing them in the name of the Father and of the Son and of the Holy Spirit, teaching them to observe all that I have commanded you. And behold, I am with you always, to the end of the age."
Matthew 28v18-20

To commission someone means to give permission, or officially charge with a task or function. Jesus sends his disciples to go. A literal translation reads more closely to make disciples *as you go*. At the most solid bedrock of this final command lies the subtly nuanced hint of the everyday-ness of the life of a disciple. The command was to saturate the world with His gospel, in His love, as a living, breathing, tangible expression of the one who sent them. You've been invited into something more. A more-ness you innately know at a soul level. A more-ness that satisfies the soul's longings and a peace that invites rest. You've been given a new identity. You have awakened from your slumber; your eyes have been opened and now you see... Go!

The apostle Paul refers to disciples of Jesus as ambassadors. An ambassador is someone who goes on behalf of someone else, someone who represents the one who sent them. With authority, in trust, on mission with specific instructions, the disciples were sent out to represent the one who sent them. Commissioned, officially charged as an ambassador, go!

Therefore, if anyone is in Christ, he is a new creation. The old has passed away; behold, the new has come. All this is from God, who through Christ reconciled us to himself and gave us the ministry of reconciliation; that is, in Christ God was reconciling the world to himself, not counting their trespasses against them, and entrusting to us the message of reconciliation. Therefore, we are ambassadors for Christ, God making his appeal through us. We implore you on behalf of Christ, be reconciled to God. For our sake he made him to be sin who knew no sin, so that in him we might become the righteousness of God.
2 Corinthians 5v17-21

Jesus commanded His disciples to go to the whole world to preach and live His gospel and make more disciples. Refreshed with new hope, full of faith, and emboldened with the Holy Spirit, the disciples preached this new message of the good news of Jesus everywhere they went. God wanted the whole world to know Him and experience His crazy, scandalous, provocative love. He commanded them to tell the story about His triumphant victory and to invite them to trust. Sin has brought inevitable death and eternal separation, but if people believe, follow, submit, and obey, they too would receive new life and experience the resurrection in their souls.

The work of renewal continues.

The work of renewal is shaped through the rhythm of missio dei.

Missio dei means the mission of God, although perhaps best understood as the God of mission. Mission is an essential characteristic and attribute of God. God has *always* been on His mission. Creation reflected His mission just as the gospel mirrors His mission. The work of renewal is shaped by His mission. God the Father sent His son Jesus to us so we could be with Him. This is the theological work of *incarnation*. God the Father and God the Son send God the Holy Spirit to dwell and make home in the people of God. The rhythm continues; the cadence grows. God the Father, God the Son, and God the Holy Spirit now send us, the people of God, His *church*, into the world.

We are the sent people of God, given the invitation to go on His behalf and represent Him.

The invitation is to join Him in His work on His mission.

The sent ones are called *missionaries*. We are sent into the world to participate in the work of renewal as God restores all things to Himself through the work of the gospel.

Missionaries live in the rhythms of the gospel.

Go.

The other day, my (David) wife took the kids to the park. Our three-year-old wanted to play with the older kids that were already there, but they obviously did not want to play with him. My son's response was to find a handful of rocks climb to the top of the largest slide and attempt to pelt the unwelcoming children with stones. He is a southpaw (a lefty) and has quite a good arm for his age, but luckily he never hit his target.

When they came home, mom filled me in on our son's target practice and I had to sit down and have a little talk with my boy. When I asked my son why he resorted to throwing rocks, he said, "I just wanted to have fun with them and they wouldn't let me." In that moment it hit me that my son has a very specific worldview. He sees the world as a playground for his own enjoyment, and every time he does not get what he wants then life is miserable. I began to think about how he has experienced life for the last three years. When his most basic needs flared up to be met, someone was always right there to meet them. His view of life is really one of being served. This was an incredible discipleship moment for us. We spent time talking about why God created us and where our joy actually comes from. I realized that he was not going to wake up one day and figure it out, and our journey as parents needed to shift from allowing him to be a consumer to teaching him how to find joy in contribution. This is why God invited Adam and Eve to be fruitful and multiply, to subdue the earth. God was inviting them to participate in co-creating.

There is an eternal joy that comes with contributing that consuming can never provide.

The rest of the night, our conversation constantly drifted back to Jesus and how He came as a blessing to the earth. He came to serve and not be served. He added value back into life's broken experiences through His contribution. For us there is a freedom in realizing that every blessing given to us becomes an eternal blessing when we use that blessing to add value to the world. It is in this idea that we are able to display the wonderful, earth-filling glory of God. This is what it means to be a sent people; we come bearing the image of God and proclaiming a message of hope. We have come to bring the better wine (John 2v1-11). We have come to bring a blessing of eternal joy. We have not come to rob others of their temporal pleasures. Sometimes I feel like, as Christians, we are more apt to be like

THERE IS AN ETERNAL JOY THAT COMES
WITH CONTRIBUTING THAT CONSUMING
CAN NEVER PROVIDE.

my son, throwing stones at the other children having fun without us. Instead, we are called to participate in the redeeming work of God so that others might find the eternal joy their hearts so desperately long for. We are not taking away but showing a better way where real joy is found. This attitude, for our children, can change their experiences in the home, elementary school, college, work, marriage, and parenting. This is the legacy of the gospel. New life and eternal joy found in participating in the glory of God.

May our children find joy in the invitation to participate in God's work in the world.

READ

Matthew 28v18-20, 9v37-38; Luke 9v1-6, 10v1-3; Colossians 4v2-6; 2 Timothy 1v9; 2 Corinthians 5v17-21; Romans 10v10-17; Acts 1v8, 8v4-25; Mark 16v15; Isaiah 6v8

MEMORIZE

Jesus sent the disciples to tell: their neighbors and the world about Him.
Jesus promised: He would always be with them.
Remember, God's love story is called: the gospel.
When people heard about the gospel: some people believed and trusted in Jesus.
These people started: following Jesus and obeying His words.

CHAT

Q: What does it mean to be sent?
A: To be sent means to go, not just to stay, but also to go tell others about Jesus and His love.

Q: When we are sent; when we GO, what are we doing?
A: Telling, sharing, and living the gospel, the love story about Jesus.

Q: Where could we share Jesus' love? Have you ever shared/told anyone about Jesus?
A: School, sports teams, neighbors. Share stories.

Q: What did we learn about God?
A: God is a sending God; He gathers and then He scatters.

Q: Where/how do we see the gospel?
A: We get to share Jesus' love with our friends; God sends because of the gospel.

PRAY

God, Your love is too big and Your grace too good to keep to ourselves. You love to make broken things new again. You love to collect broken pieces and make beautiful things. Thank you for making things new. Give us the courage to tell, share, and show Your love to our neighbors and friends so they will know that Your love holds everything together. Amen.

JESUS SENT THE DISCIPLES TO TELL **THEIR NEIGHBORS** AND THE WORLD ABOUT HIM.

JESUS PROMISED **HE WOULD ALWAYS BE WITH THEM.**

REMEMBER GOD'S LOVES STORY IS CALLED **THE GOSPEL.**

WHEN PEOPLE HEARD ABOUT THE GOSPEL **SOME PEOPLE BELIEVED AND TRUSTED IN JESUS.**

THESE PEOPLE STARTED **FOLLOWING JESUS** AND OBEYING HIS WORDS.

18
THE CHURCH

The work of the gospel is the work of renewal and restoration here and now. It is the compass that points us back home. The gospel satisfies the garden longings that lie as a remnant upon the beating hearts of humanity. The work of Jesus revives the dormant purposes set deep within the hearts of humanity in creation and gives us foretastes of Eden now, in the midst of the pain and suffering of the human condition. We taste samples of peace now. Like the calling of Eden, the gospel invites us to join Him in His work, on His mission, again. Created in the image of the creator, given dominion and authority to steward over creation, the invitation was to mirror the heart of God back to creation. Lead and serve, create with me, let the breath of your nostrils and the work of your hands be an expression of love, an exclamation of worship. The gospel reestablishes the original intent of God: humans as image bearers of the divine community created from more, for more. Now, because of the birth, life, death, and resurrection of Jesus, we are rescued by Jesus, through Jesus, for Jesus, to be with God again. The gospel reestablishes *imago dei* and now sends us out into the world to show the world who the creator is and what He is like again. The creator breathed His spirit into the dust of the ground and life emerged. Now, through the gospel, we receive the Holy Spirit, and new life blossoms from the dust again. God, the master artist, the grand storyteller, is beautifully and magnificently exposing the lies of the adversary and placing truth back in the hearts of His people.

...you will receive power when the Holy Spirit has come upon you, and you will be my witnesses in Jerusalem and in all Judea and Samaria, and to the end of the earth."
Acts 1v8

"You will be my witnesses" are the last words Jesus spoke to His disciples before He ascended into the fullness of His glory to be with His father. Jesus came to be with us so that we could be with Him. This is the essence of incarnation. The fullness of God dwelled among us, showing the world who He is and what He is like. The incarnation was necessary for rescue, and now Jesus invites his disciples to go and do the same in the world. Invited to join Jesus and be His students, schooling is over. A thousand days of Jesus University prepared them for this moment; go, be my witnesses physically and tangibly. As my witnesses, tell the world my story. Tell them what you've seen; tell them what you've heard. Show them my love, and let them see how it looks.

Oh, taste and see that the LORD is good!
Psalm 34v8

These witnesses have been with Jesus, walked with Jesus, experienced miracles, heard sermons; their entire worlds have been turned upside down since the first invitation to "follow me." They didn't just know about Jesus, they were there *with* Him. They didn't follow from a distance, at their own leisure for their own pleasure; they were there in every moment. They learned to pray, to preach, to serve, to trust, to depend. Jesus prepared them for the way ahead and promised, "I am with you always."

The authorities from the religious sect and from the Roman Empire wouldn't take the news of the message of Jesus multiplying, lightly. Their efforts to thwart the *Jesus Way* only sparked more intrigue and brought more attention. The fire was lit and burning more brightly than ever, but more attention brought more trouble for the Jesus followers. For fear of insurrection and rebellion, the Roman authorities and Jewish leaders tried to snuff out the fire. Persecution broke out against the early Jesus followers, at this point referred to as Christians in their culture, a term that exists in our day throughout the world. More persecution, more trouble, and further attempts to marginalize the early Christians and ostracize their communities only created further belief in their message. The number of Jesus's disciples was growing.

Amidst the myriad of early opposition to the newly formed Jesus Way was one particular man with a deep-seated hatred for the movement. His name was Saul. He was a Pharisee, one of the Jewish teachers and protectors of the law. Pharisees claimed Mosaic authority for their interpretation of Jewish law according to Torah, the first five books of the Old Testament (Genesis, Exodus, Leviticus, Numbers, and Deuteronomy). Tasked with holding the Jewish people true to the law, Saul upheld the letter of the law with vigilant zeal. He writes a brief description of himself in the letter written to the Church at Philippi:

Circumcised on the eighth day, of the people of Israel, of the tribe of Benjamin, a Hebrew of Hebrews; as to the law, a Pharisee; as to zeal, a persecutor of the church; as to righteousness under the law, blameless.
Philippians 3v5-6

Saul was a scholar, the best of the best and the brightest of all his colleagues. He was on a mission to oppose, prevent, and obstruct the movement and message of Jesus from advancing, at any cost. His reputation of ruthlessness toward Christians and their message was known everywhere. All those who held their allegiance to Jesus were in his crosshairs. Saul was vehemently opposed to the gospel, but the power of the gospel was too strong to stymie.

But Saul, still breathing threats and murder against the disciples of the Lord, went to the high priest and asked him for letters to the synagogues at Damascus, so that if he found any belonging to the Way, men or women, he might bring them bound to Jerusalem.
Acts 9v1-2

The faithful father always pursues. Jesus met Saul on the road to Damascus that day. Luke writes in the book of Acts that a bright light from heaven blinded Saul and a voice from above invited Saul into a new way forward. God chose Saul as an "instrument to carry his name" further than the gospel had ever been preached. The saving power of the gospel completely transformed the man known as Saul. He began to preach and proclaim Jesus and plant the seeds of the gospel everywhere he went. He encouraged believers and partnered with them to take the gospel message of Jesus into new frontiers and among new peoples. Where Christians were sent, the gospel was preached, the gospel was heard, and the gospel was believed.

How then will they call on him in whom they have not believed? And how are they to believe in him of whom they have never heard? And how are they to hear without someone preaching? And how are they to preach unless they are sent? As it is written, "How beautiful are the feet of those who preach the good news!"
Romans 10v14-15

The gospel was being preached and lived, disciples were being multiplied, and vibrant communities of believers were blooming all over. From the seeds of the gospel, new communities of followers all over the known world were emerging. These communities of believers in the first century came to be known as the *ekklesia*. It comes from two Greek words that mean "the called out ones." This is the word that we translate as *church*. The church, which is to say *the people of God*, rises from the seeds of the planted gospel. Obedient to the call to go and preach, the church became a family of missionaries, commissioned to love and serve the world every day, everywhere, all the time. It was a community within a larger community whose function and purpose was to bring the rhythms of the kingdom of God to their communities. The role of the church is humble participation in God's work in the world.

The biblical emphasis of the church is based on our new identity in the gospel. Because we have been loved, we love. We have been blessed, so we bless. We display the fruit of the spirit actively at work in us as bringers and extenders of love, joy, peace, patience, kindness, goodness, gentleness, and self-control. Through love and unity, the world will get a glimpse of the father. The church is God's chosen people, distinct, His family set apart to live and engage in such a way that the world takes notice. Out of His untamed, magnificent love, the father sends His son to show the world the father's love. Out of that same love, He now sends the church to show the father's love.

We are called out ... as distinct.
Invited to engage ... as restorers.
Sent to love ... as family.

The work of renewal continues.
As the church, we join God in the renewal of all things.

You are the light of the world. A city set on a hill cannot be hidden. Nor do people light a lamp and put it under a basket, but on a stand, and it gives light to all in the house. In the same way, let your light shine before others, so that they may see your good works and give glory to your Father who is in heaven.
Matthew 5v14-16

There is, perhaps, no greater motivator than an intrinsic sense of purpose. From the time my children could talk, they were dreaming about what they would be when they grow up. A firefighter, veterinarian, shop owner, football player, professional Lego tower builder. We have heard it all and have spent countless nights laughing and dreaming about what they would do one day. *At the heart of all the dreaming is a desire for significance.* A genuine desire to want to contribute to the world in a significant way. We know the age-old question, "Why do we exist?". It has haunted humanity since the beginning of existence. For our children, this question will also haunt them, and every culture has its own answer. As the church, we are called out of our culture's purposes and returned back to God's eternal design for creation. We, as His people, now live distinct and set apart lives so that God would be recognized for who He is, what He has done, and what He promises to do. We are called out of darkness and into marvelous light so that the excellency of Christ can be proclaimed through us to the world around us and the glory of God might once again be seen in His most beloved creation. We are distinct, yes, but we are called to engage our world. We are not separatists, nor conformists, but invited to be transformists in our communities. His church is part of His plan to once again fill His earth with His glory.

A beautiful part of the discipling relationship we get to have with our children is helping them see a bigger vision for why they exist. We get to help them see what it means to be God's people living for God's glory. The tragedy for our children is that Church has often times been reduced to a few-hours-per-week activity where adults sing and listen to a person lecture them and the kids get sectored away to play cheesy Bible games and listen to flowery flannel graph stories. This oftentimes will leave them looking to the world to find a more significant purpose and a more fulfilling identity. Although gathering with other believers, being unified in song, sitting under the preaching of the word, and celebrating communion as a faith family are all beautiful privileges for the Christian, we have to make sure our children see church as who they are and not what they do. It is their identity, not a religious, rote, mechanical activity. The Church is a people whose hearts have been raptured by God's love -- a love that set in motion invitation to participate in the redeeming purposes of God's eternal glory. We are light to a dark world and hope to a hopeless people. Setting this purpose deep in the hearts of our children will be a life-long work of love, discipleship, and prayer.

May our children find a life of significance in the eternal purpose found in Jesus.

READ

1 Peter 2v9-11; Colossians 1v21-23, 3v15; Acts 2v42-47; Ephesians 1v3-14, 4v4; Romans 12v4-5, 12v10-13 15v6-7; 1 Corinthians 1v9, 12v12-31; Matthew 12v49-50, 1 John 3v1-24, 4v7; Psalms 133v1-3; Hebrews 10v24-25

MEMORIZE

Jesus came to be with us so: we could be with God.
People who follow Jesus are called: disciples.
These disciples: live life together.
Disciples who live life together are called: the church.
The church is: God's family.

CHAT

Q: What were the disciples sent to do?
A: Preach the gospel; live the life of love; show Jesus to their family, friends, neighbors, co-workers, and the world by living life together for the gospel.

Q: How do disciples live life together?
A: Share in life's rhythms: eat, celebrate, bless, mourn, serve, learn, teach (Acts 2v42-47).

Q: What, or better said, who is the church?
A: Disciples together are the church. (If we are the church, can we "go" to church?)

Q: What did we learn about God?
A: God, first and foremost, is a father; God desires unity and togetherness; God is making a family.

Q: Where/how do we see the gospel?
A: Without Jesus, we are not sons and daughters, brothers and sisters; we are family because of Jesus.

PRAY

God, You are the perfect father. You sent Jesus, the perfect son, to show the world Your love. You invited us to be with You and to live life with the people who are with You, Your church. There is no togetherness outside of You, no unity apart from Your love.

JESUS CAME TO BE WITH US SO **WE COULD BE WITH GOD.**

PEOPLE WHO FOLLOW JESUS ARE CALLED **DISCIPLES.**

THESE DISCIPLES **LIVE LIFE TOGETHER.**

DISCIPLES WHO LIVE LIFE TOGETHER ARE CALLED **THE CHURCH.**

THE CHURCH IS **GOD'S FAMILY.**

19
EVERYDAY LOVE

...that they should seek God, and perhaps feel their way toward him and find him. Yet he is actually not far from each one of us, for "'In him we live and move and have our being'; as even some of your own poets have said, "'For we are indeed his offspring.'
Acts 17v27-28

Simple yet profound words: I love you. The Father sends the Son to show the Father's love, and through grace, the Father invites us to be with Him. This is where the church gets its identity and where the movement of love begins. We have been welcomed into more, invited into belonging, and ushered into God's family. It's from this identity that we set out to live.

From the beginning, the church was more than a place, more than a moment, more than a weekend or midweek stop; the church is a community of people who participate in the way of Jesus and His work in the world—to reclaim, redeem, and restore everything on earth as it is in heaven. Each part is valuable and necessary for the whole body to function properly. The church in the New Testament, was an ordinary group of people who became a dynamic community of believers centered on the gospel. These new communities embodied the tangible family of God together. They moved like family, lived like family, took care of one another like family, sacrificed for one another like family, and served like family. Together the world would see who God is and what He is like. Like a body with many members and many parts that collectively construct a whole, together we, as family, though individuals, collectively make up the church.

For as in one body we have many members, and the members do not all have the same function, so we, though many, are one body in Christ, and individually members one of another.
Romans 12v4-5

And they devoted themselves to the apostles' teaching and the fellowship, to the breaking of bread and the prayers. And awe came upon every soul, and many wonders and signs were being done through the apostles. And all who believed

were together and had all things in common. And they were selling their possessions
and belongings and distributing the proceeds to all, as any had need. And day
by day, attending the temple together and breaking bread in their homes, they
received their food with glad and generous hearts, praising God and having favor
with all the people. And the Lord added to their number day by day those who were
being saved.
Acts 2v42-47

From this radical togetherness, new believers experienced the gospel, and authentic community emerged. The scriptures tell stories of the early church consistently eating together, worshipping together, praying together, learning together, and sacrificing for each other. Simply put, because of the work of the gospel and the church's devotion to God, its members became devoted to one another. Jesus set a new standard and gave His disciples a new way to live and love. We are to love in the same way and to the same extent that He has loved us. We sacrificially serve one another as He sacrificially served us. In this way, the world experiences an authentic, visible, and accessible expression of community. The church is this expression, and it cannot be manufactured or fabricated. There is no assembly line for family. It goes beyond a paint-by-the-numbers prescription. It's messy. It's hard. It confronts the corruption in our hearts and exposes our selfishness. Togetherness reveals our idols and shows the gaping holes in our unbelief. We were created for community, and we were never intended to live outside of it. We long at a primal depth to be part of something.

Remember the communal language from Eden? "Let *us* make man in *our* image... in *our* likeness he created them." Part of being human is living life with other humans. The *imago dei* is seen in radical togetherness. The church is the invitation to not be alone. The gospel confronts our radical individualistic western reality and invites us into belonging. As we drift from community, we naturally drift from love; thus community grips us in love's proximity. When we live in proximity and intimacy with God, we learn to love ourselves, develop healthy relationships, and become passionate about loving other people. But when we grow distant from God and disconnected from community, we discover that we become increasingly emptied of love. An exile of the heart takes place. This can tend to lead us on a trajectory to unhealthy dependence on people. We can't fully depend on other people. That's like brokenness depending on brokenness; we can wholly hope, trust, and depend on the gospel alone. The church is the incarnation of the gospel, and now, the gospel lives and is active in other people. The church goes into the everyday rhythms of the world and saturates the corners of the culture in truth and love. The church, in flesh and bone, with blood in our veins and gospel on our lips, with opens hands and stretched out arms, joins God in the renewal of His creation. From gospel seeds, real community naturally emerges out of love.

"A new commandment I give to you, that you love one another: just as I have loved you, you also are to love one another. By this all people will know that you are my disciples, if you have love for one another."
John 13v34-35

Let's connect all the dots: as the truth of the gospel takes root in our lives and reshapes our identities, we are given a purpose outside of ourselves. Saved by God's work, for God's work, we are given a calling bigger than our individualism, and humility becomes the natural echo in our lives. In humble participation with God on His mission, we are sent into the world.

God sends us to light the world.

As a family of missionaries sent to show the father's love, engagement requires an attentive ear and receptive heart to know how to respond. So we listen. We listen so that we may become aware and understand the people, places, rhythms and stories of our communities. We listen so that we may demonstrate and declare His love to the world. To be sent is the normal posture of the church. Sent-ness is the normal disposition of the people of God. Biblically, there exists this reality that the more deeply we experience and know the depth of love that the father has for us, the more we naturally develop a deep affection for the people that God has placed in our lives. The deeper the love of God envelops our souls, the more we love people.

Therefore be imitators of God, as beloved children. And walk in love, as Christ loved us and gave himself up for us, a fragrant offering and sacrifice to God.
Ephesians 5v1-2

Love engages.

Love gets involved.

The love of Christ renews, rebuilds, and restores.

Now, the church is invited to fill our cities, our neighborhoods, our villages, our schools, and every corner of our culture with the presence of Christ, continually showing God to a broken world.

Like arrows in the hand of a warrior are the children of one's youth. Blessed is the man who fills his quiver with them! He shall not be put to shame when he speaks with his enemies in the gate.
Psalm 127v4-5

Before I met Jesus I was filled with confusion, bitterness, loneliness, and--quite frankly--boredom. I could not find rest; there was an angst that burned deep inside which nothing could quench; then Jesus saved me. It was like someone turned a switch on in my heart. Where there was once bitterness and anger, there is now an undiscovered capacity to love and be loved. It truly was a miracle!

I never imagined God's love would open up a world of endless possibilities.

Love changes everything; it creates space for rest and produces energy for life. It heals wounds and comforts pains. The love of Christ constrains us to push on toward the upward call of God in Christ. Where there was once rebellion, there is now desire. His love, that which was poured into my heart, transformed me from death to life. I remember so clearly seeing His love as the motivation that carried Him to His cross. It was His love that whispered the truth I desperately longed to hear -- "He is clean, holy, righteous, forgiven; he is mine." In Christ I could hear the Father's voice say of me what He said of His son: "This is my beloved son, in whom I am well pleased." Love is a very powerful thing. When unleashed, it has the power to turn the world upside down.

Jesus begins His ministry on the earth armed with the love of the Father. Everything He does from that moment is done from His identity as loved and accepted by God. This is what I want for my children. I want them to be sent out into the world, shot like arrows, every day

LOVE ENGAGES.

LOVE GETS INVOLVED.

knowing both my love and approval of them and God's love and approval of them. A type of assurance that cannot easily be ripped from their hearts. The more I understand God's love for me and the basis for His approval, the more I am able to love my children and guide them to Christ. When I think of the primary posture I take in parenting, it is mostly a defensive posture. I want to keep my children safe both from the world and themselves. I want to arm my children with the necessary armor to keep them from experiencing life's pains and traps. Most of the time, my parenting style is equivalent to the mother in 'A Christmas Story' bundling up her youngest son to the point of immobility. He can barely lift an arm as he is sent out into a cold and bitter world. No, he will not catch a cold, but he is bound up so tightly that he is unable to contribute to society in any sort of meaningful way. He just exists in his protective cocoon watching life pass him by. Although arming our children with the tools necessary to withstand life's most basic evils is not bad, on its own *it is not enough*. What I want most is to teach my children how to love and be loved. How to look at the world through the lens of God's heart. The sacrifice of Jesus is not a one-time lottery. It is the very heart of God towards His creation, every day, all the time, in every moment. When our children begin to see the depth of God's love, their little rebellious hearts melts and their souls are armed to live new life as a gift to the world. A testimony of God's grace, a beacon of hope, and a display of His great love. Our identity as God's beloved children is what motivates new life without fear of death.

May we walk close to the Father as we walk out into the world.

READ

1 Timothy 6v17-19; John 13v34-35, 15v12-13; 2 Corinthians 5v17-21; 1 John 3v15-16, 4v7-8; 1 Corinthians 13v1-13, 16v14; Galatians 5v22; Ephesians 5v1; 1 Thessalonians 3v12; 1 Peter 4v8; Matthew 7v1-5; Colossians 3v12-15; Hebrews 13v1-3

MEMORIZE

Now the church lives all around the world sharing the gospel: with its neighbors.
The church has been invited to: join God.
The church shares the gospel by: loving neighbors and serving them.
Jesus tells us to love one another like: He loves us.
When we love each other: the world sees how Jesus loves.

CHAT

Q: Where is the church?
A: Everywhere. We bring gospel everywhere we go, in the rhythms of the church.

Q: How do we share the gospel with our neighbors?
A: By serving them and loving them; inviting them to join us in living life together.

Q: How do our neighbors get to see the gospel in the everyday rhythms of life?
A: By the way the church loves one another, cares for one another, serves one another.

Q: What did we learn about God?
A: God uses us, broken people, to show His love to the world; God invites us to join Him in representing who He is to the world.

Q: Where/how do we see the gospel?
A: We cannot represent God without God first inviting us; we cannot pursue the world without God first pursuing us.

PRAY

God, Your love is limitless and boundless. You came here to show us love, real love, true love, perfect love through Your son Jesus. The depths of the oceans and the heights of the mountains cannot contain Your love. The colorful hues and the vibrant sounds of Your creation are merely glimpses of You. May our love for one another be a radiant glimpse of who You are and how You love. May our love show that Your love holds everything together. Amen.

NOW THE CHURCH LIVES ALL AROUND THE WORLD SHARING THE GOSPEL

WITH THEIR NEIGHBORS.

THE CHURCH HAS BEEN INVITED TO

JOIN GOD.

THE CHURCH SHARES THE GOSPEL BY

LOVING NEIGHBORS AND SERVING THEM.

JESUS TELLS US TO LOVE ONE ANOTHER LIKE

HE LOVES US.

WHEN WE LOVE EACH OTHER,

THE WORLD

SEES HOW JESUS LOVES.

20
RETURN

LORD, I have heard of your fame; I stand in awe of your deeds, LORD.
Renew them in our day, in our time make them known; in wrath remember mercy.
The prayer of the prophet Habakkuk

"And that is precisely what Christianity is about. The world is a great sculptor's shop.
We are the statues and there is a rumor going round the shop that some of us are
some day are going to come to life."
C. S. Lewis[1]

Things have gone awry and humanity continues to move further away from who we were created to be and where we were created to live. The famine in our souls swells as we look to exist east of Eden. Every attempt to satisfy the longing is like trying to sneak back into the garden. But we are in exile, stuck in a never-ending cycle of longing for our home. Even when we get a taste, it never quenches; it never lasts. The great lie distorted everything and the adversary has been on the prowl ever since spinning his version of the story. Weaving distorted truth into his already overflowing tapestry of lies, he seeks to steal, kill, and destroy.

Slow and subtle death oftentimes is the most dangerous -- the kind of death that lurks subterranean, deep enough below the surface that on most days we can't smell its stench. It's the kind of decay that gradually leads us into isolation. Unaware of our subtle drift, we eventually end up in a place of deep loneliness. Cynicism says this is as good as it gets. This life, here and now, is your best shot at happiness and fulfillment. The allure of Eden is nothing but a mirage of more. With our expectations rarely met, disappointment becomes the norm of the human condition. But the soul never stops searching. It's designed to belong; it's designed to love and to be loved. We were created for more.

He has made everything beautiful in its time. Also, he has put eternity into man's heart,
yet so that he cannot find out what God has done from the beginning to the end.
Ecclesiastes 3v11

The story is far from over.

There is still more.

The thief comes only to steal and kill and destroy. I came that they may have life and have it abundantly.
John 10v10

In fact, the enemy has already been defeated, and everything is moving toward resurrection. Everything is moving toward restoration and renewal, where everything will be put back into its right and proper place.

The triumphal defeat over the grave was the victorious blow to Satan and his schemes. The gospel announces that we have been saved from penalty of sin, that we are being saved from the power of sin, and that we will be saved from the presence of sin. This is the promise of the gospel. The gospel is the proclamation that Satan's conquest has been defeated and the reign and rule of Christ is at hand. The apostle Paul illustrates this poignantly in his letter to the church in Ephesus.

...and what is the immeasurable greatness of his power toward us who believe, according to the working of his great might that he worked in Christ when he raised him from the dead and seated him at his right hand in the heavenly places, far above all rule and authority and power and dominion, and above every name that is named, not only in this age but also in the one to come. And he put all things under his feet and gave him as head over all things to the church, which is his body, the fullness of him who fills all in all.
Ephesians 1v19b-23

Since that tragic moment in the garden, when Eve took the bait and took the bite, the story has always been moving toward resurrection, moving toward renewal and restoration. As we have clearly seen, the path to new life is through Jesus. Jesus boldly claims, "I am the way, and the truth, and the life. No one comes to the Father except through me. If you had known me, you would have known my Father also. From now on you do know Him and have seen Him" (John 14v6-7). Jesus declares that He is the conduit through which we get to the father. Our garden longings can only be satisfied in and through Jesus. Return from exile is only possible through grace, through faith in the person and work of Jesus. The apostle Paul refers to this as the ministry of reconciliation. Our rebellion and sin caused just enmity with God, the faithful and holy father. Our sin separated us from God and the chasm is too expansive to navigate. As covenant maker and covenant keeper, God is perpetually faithful. As broken and unfaithful, we are perpetually unable to keep covenant. God's holy and righteous standard is too great for us to meet, too high for us to reach; it must be fulfilled. Paul beautifully articulates how Jesus extravagantly accommodated us, His beloved, and welcomed us back home.

And you, who once were alienated and hostile in mind, doing evil deeds, he has now reconciled in his body of flesh by his death, in order to present you holy and blameless and above reproach before him, if indeed you continue in the faith, stable and steadfast, not shifting from the hope of the gospel that you heard, which has been proclaimed in all creation under heaven, and of which I, Paul, became a minister.
Colossians 1v21-23

Therefore, if anyone is in Christ, he is a new creation. The old has passed away; behold, the new has come. All this is from God, who through Christ reconciled us to himself and gave us the ministry of reconciliation; that is, in Christ God was reconciling the world to himself, not counting their trespasses against them, and entrusting to us the message of reconciliation. Therefore, we are ambassadors for Christ, God making his appeal through us. We implore you on behalf of Christ, be reconciled to God. For our sake he made him to be sin who knew no sin, so that in him we might become the righteousness of God.
2 Corinthians 5v18-21

In Ephesians, Paul refers to Jesus as our peace: "But now in Christ Jesus you who once were far off have been brought near by the blood of Christ. For He Himself is our peace" (Ephesians 2:13-14a). This word for peace carries the same idea as reconciliation. It is a picture of union, and it connotes binding together or joining that which is broken and in need of repair. Jesus is our mediator. The prophet Isaiah calls the coming messiah a prince of peace. Jesus not only mediates on our behalf, but as the prince of peace, he is the maintainer of peace.

As mediator, Jesus is the giver of grace.
As maintainer, Jesus is the bringer of peace.

And he shall be their peace.
Micah 5v5

We are holy, blameless, above reproach and God is not counting our sin against us, and withholding our rebellion. Since we no longer live in exile, the journey home is possible. Restoration is available. Return is hopeful. Keeping consistent with His character and nature, God invites the reconciled to join Him again, trusting us as His representatives. This is mind-blowing! The earthly ministry of Jesus has been entrusted to and given to His church.

In Eden, the created were invited to join in creating.

Through the gospel, the reconciled become reconcilers.

Invited to join in the great campaign of renewal, the once-broken seek to bring wholeness.

The scriptures tell of a coming time when there will be no more slavery, no more exile, and no more bondage, but freedom, liberty, and renewal will be our song. Jesus said, "I go to prepare a place for you. And if I go and prepare a place for you, I will come again and will take you to myself, that where I am you may be also" (John 14v2-3). We have glimpses of peace now, a sense of with-ness here, bite-sized reminders of more. There is a presence of peace, but there is still a promise of more. Shalom is coming again. In fullness and completeness, everything will be in its right and proper place again.

"The Spirit of the Lord is upon me, because he has anointed me to proclaim good news to the poor. He has sent me to proclaim liberty to the captives and recovering of sight to the blind, to set at liberty those who are oppressed."
Luke 4v18

Sin has been defeated.
Rumors of resurrection are true.
New life is possible.

He has created.
He is creating.
He will recreate.

EDEN WAS GOOD.

JESUS IS BETTER.

JESUS IS THE BETTER EDEN.

Then I saw a new heaven and a new earth, for the first heaven and the first earth had passed away, and the sea was no more. And I saw the holy city, new Jerusalem, coming down out of heaven from God, prepared as a bride adorned for her husband. And I heard a loud voice from the throne saying, "Behold, the dwelling place of God is with man. He will dwell with them, and they will be his people, and God himself will be with them as their God. He will wipe away every tear from their eyes, and death shall be no more, neither shall there be mourning, nor crying, nor pain anymore, for the former things have passed away." And he who was seated on the throne said, **"Behold, I am making all things new."**
Revelation 21v1-5

The scriptures end with a dramatic revelation given to the disciple known as John. A vision from God shared with John to be shared with humanity to give us hope. Perhaps this is to further illustrate His faithfulness, as echoed by the words of the prophet Jeremiah, "For I know the plans I have for you, declares the LORD, plans for welfare and not for evil, to give you a future and a hope" (Jeremiah 29v11). This revelation is the promised hope for the beloved.

The revelation is a vision that God has been sharing with humanity from the beginning. A wedding feast. Jesus as the bridegroom, beckoning His bride, the church to come. Adorned in white, clothed in righteousness, full of love; intimacy awaits. Before the great lie, the man and the woman were without shame, and again we will no longer know the consequences of the fall.

My beloved speaks and says to me: 'Arise, my love, my beautiful one, and come away.'
Song of Solomon 2v10

Eternity isn't about Eden... The story has never been about Eden. The garden in the beginning, and the echoes of Eden since, have always been about Jesus. The whispers of eternity have always been Jesus. His story is about the hero.

Eden was good.
> *Jesus is better.*
>> *Jesus is the better Eden.*
>>> *We were created to know Him.*
>>>> *This is His story, may it be told in our*
>>>>> *homes for generations to come.*

READ

Jeremiah 29v11, 30v17, 31v12; Isaiah 58v11; 2 Corinthians 3v15-18; Romans 14v11; Joel 2v25-26; Acts 3v21; Matthew 24v36; Revelation 21v1-5; John 10v10; Psalms 23v1-6, 71v20-21, 103v1-5; 1 Peter 5v10

MEMORIZE

Through Jesus, God is reestablishing: peace.
Through Jesus, God is bringing: freedom.
Through Jesus, God is: renewing His creation.
Through Jesus, God is putting everything back in its: right and proper place.
And through Jesus, once again: it is very good.

CHAT

Q: Where is freedom found?
A: In Jesus alone. Through obedience and love, we find rest in Jesus.

Q: Is everything as it should be? Is everything in its right and proper place?
A: No. What's not right with the world? Sickness; war; sadness; pain.

Q: Where and when was everything right? How will everything be right again?
A: Eden; before deception and sin. Jesus is renewing and and restoring all things. Through Jesus, everything will obey God; everything will bow in submission to Jesus (again).

Q: What did we learn about God?
A: God desires freedom and loves for His children to experience freedom. God is freedom. God loves to make things new again.

Q: Where/how do we see the gospel?
A: Jesus and the work of the cross are the means of reconciliation, the means of peace, the means by which everything finds its place again in the created order.

PRAY

God, from the beginning, You created everything out of Your love and for Your glory. You created all things as a reflection of who You are... Body, soul, and spirit... Love, family, and unity... Everything so we could know You and be with You. Through Your son Jesus, You are making everything new again. The puzzle is complete, no missing pieces. The ripple effects of love are greater than the ripple effects of sin. Your love alone holds everything together. Amen.

THROUGH JESUS, GOD IS REESTABLISHING

PEACE.

THROUGH JESUS, GOD IS BRINGING

FREEDOM.

THROUGH JESUS, GOD IS
RENEWING HIS CREATION.

THROUGH JESUS, GOD IS PUTTING EVERYTHING BACK IN ITS
RIGHT AND PROPER PLACE.

AND THROUGH JESUS, ONCE AGAIN
IT IS VERY GOOD.

BENEDICTION

For this reason, because I have heard of your faith in the Lord Jesus and your love toward all the saints, I do not cease to give thanks for you, remembering you in my prayers, that the God of our Lord Jesus Christ, the Father of glory, may give you the Spirit of wisdom and of revelation in the knowledge of him, having the eyes of your hearts enlightened, that you may know what is the hope to which he has called you, what are the riches of his glorious inheritance in the saints, and what is the immeasurable greatness of his power toward us who believe, according to the working of his great might that he worked in Christ when he raised him from the dead and seated him at his right hand in the heavenly places, far above all rule and authority and power and dominion, and above every name that is named, not only in this age but also in the one to come. And he put all things under his feet and gave him as head over all things to the church, which is his body, the fullness of him who fills all in all.
Ephesians 1v15-23

For this reason I bow my knees before the Father, from whom every family in heaven and on earth is named, that according to the riches of his glory he may grant you to be strengthened with power through his Spirit in your inner being, so that Christ may dwell in your hearts through faith-that you, being rooted and grounded in love, may have strength to comprehend with all the saints what is the breadth and length and height and depth, and to know the love of Christ that surpasses knowledge, that you may be filled with all the fullness of God. Now to him who is able to do far more abundantly than all that we ask or think, according to the power at work within us, to him be glory in the church and in Christ Jesus throughout all generations, forever and ever. Amen.
Ephesians 3v14-21

CREATION

GOD

The beginning of the story is called: creation.

The creator is: God.

God is: perfect.

God created: everything.

God created everything: out of love and for His glory.

EDEN

At the beginning of the story there is a: garden.

The garden is called: Eden.

Eden was a place where everything was in its: right and proper place.

And God said: it is good.

It was good because: God is good and He was there.

HUMANITY

God's most special creation was: man and woman.

Their names were: Adam and Eve.

They were special because: they were created in God's image.

To be created in God's image means: to represent Him and glorify Him.

And then God said: it is very good.

TOGETHER

It was God's desire that man and woman would always: be with Him and take care of His creation.

God would always: love Adam and Eve and take care of them.

Because God was faithful, God would always: provide everything they needed.

Eden was home because: God was with them.

God was in control and had: complete authority.

PERFECTION

They trusted God and: believed in Him.

Adam and Eve loved God so they: obeyed Him.

In love and obedience: there is always freedom.

Eden was: perfect and complete.

God was their: everything.

REBELLION

THE ADVERSARY

Everything was good but: everything was about to change.

The most deceitful, crafty, and tricky animal in the garden was: the serpent.

The serpent was: the enemy (Satan means adversary).

The serpent deceived Adam and Eve into thinking that they didn't: need God anymore.

But that wasn't true, was it? – That's called: a lie.

THE GREAT LIE

Unfortunately, Adam and Eve: believed the lie.

Any time we don't trust and believe in God, that's called: sin.

When we sin, that's called: disobedience.

All of sin is: rebellion.

But God's grand design is: love.

THE SHAME

Remember, there is always freedom in: love and obedience.

But Adam and Eve: disobeyed.

All sin produces: shame and separation.

When we sin, we hurt the heart of God: because God loves us.

So Adam and Eve tried to: cover their own shame.

THE CONSEQUENCE

Because Adam and Eve sinned: everything changed.

Adam and Eve: forgot.

God is holy and always does what is: good, right, and perfect.

Because God is holy, He does not allow: sin to be in His presence.

God punished Adam and Eve by: removing them from the garden (His presence).

THE DESPERATION

Adam and Eve were now: sinners.

As hard as they tried, Adam and Eve could not fix: what was broken.

They never stopped: needing God.

And God would never stop: loving them.

But the story doesn't: end there.

GOSPEL

THE GREAT RESCUE

God's love is: bigger and better than sin.

God would never stop: pursuing His creation (us).

God's love story is about: Jesus.

God's love story about Jesus is called: the gospel.

The gospel means that Jesus came to: rescue us.

GRACE

Jesus came to rescue us so that we could: know Him.

We can know Him because He gives us: grace.

He gives us grace even though we: don't deserve it.

We don't deserve it because of: our sin/rebellion.

Sin separates, but Jesus brings us back: home with God.

HOLINESS

We are all broken and full of sin, but: Jesus has never sinned.

He has never sinned because: He is holy.

To be holy means: to be set apart.

To be set apart means: to be like God.

To be like God means: to be righteous and perfect.

JESUS IS BETTER

Jesus had to be holy, righteous, and perfect in order to: rescue us.

Jesus' perfection: covers our sin.

He rescued us by: dying on a cross.

But three days later: He rose from the grave.

He came back to life because: God's love is bigger and better than sin.

BELONGING

Remember, it is God's desire that man and woman would always: be with Him.

So Jesus never stops: pursuing.

Jesus puts the broken pieces: back together.

And offers us: rest and belonging.

Jesus is the way: back home.

RECREATION

MULTIPLY

God wanted the whole world: to know Him.

And to know: His love.

The first people who knew Jesus were called: His disciples.

The disciples: followed Jesus everywhere.

After the resurrection, God would greatly multiply: the number of disciples.

THE SENT ONES

Jesus sent the disciples to tell: their neighbors and the world about Him.

Jesus promised: He would always be with them.

Remember, God's love story is called: the gospel.

When people heard about the gospel: some people believed and trusted in Jesus.

These people started: following Jesus and obeying His words.

THE CHURCH

Jesus came to be with us so: we could be with God.

People who follow Jesus are called: disciples.

These disciples: live life together.

Disciples who live life together are called: the church.

The church is: God's family.

EVERYDAY LOVE

Now the church lives all around the world sharing the gospel: with its neighbors.

The church has been invited to: join God.

The church shares the gospel by: loving neighbors and serving them.

Jesus tells us to love one another like: He loves us.

When we love each other: the world sees how Jesus loves.

RETURN

Through Jesus, God is reestablishing: peace.

Through Jesus, God is bringing: freedom.

Through Jesus, God is: renewing His creation.

Through Jesus, God is putting everything back in its: right and proper place.

And through Jesus, once again: it is very good.

NOTES

QUOTE 1:
1.) C.S. Lewis, Mere Christianity (San Francisco: Harper, 1980)

THE JOURNEY:
1.) G. K. Chesterton, What's Wrong With the World (CreateSpace Indepen- dent Publishing Platform, 2009)
2.) Curtis, Brent, and John Eldredge. The Sacred Romance: Drawing Closer to the Heart of God. Nashville: Thomas Nelson, 1997.
3.) A. W. Tozer, The Knowledge of the Holy (New York, NY: Harper Collins Publishers, 1961)

INSTRUCTIONS:
1.) A. W. Tozer, The Pursuit of God (Harrisburg, PA: Christian Publications, 1948)
2.) A. W. Tozer, The Pursuit of God (Harrisburg, PA: Christian Publications, 1948)

CREATION:
1.) G. K. Chesterton, Orthodoxy (New York: John Lane Company; London, 1908)
2.) Drew Dyck, Yawning at Tigers (Nashville, TN: Thomas Nelson, 2014)
3.) Manning, Brennan. The Furious Longing of God. Colorado Springs, CO: David C. Cook, 2009.
4.) C. S. Lewis, The Lion, the Witch and the Wardrobe (United Kingdom: Geoffrey Bles, 1950)
5.) Eugene Peterson, The Jesus Way: A Conversation on the Ways That Jesus Is the Way (Wm. B. Eerdmans Publishing Co.; Reprint edition 2011)
6.) Brent Curtis and John Eldredge, The Sacred Romance (Nashville, TN: Thomas Nelson, 1997)

7.) C. S. Lewis, Mere Christianity (New York: HarperCollins e-books, 2009)
8.) Zack Eswine, Sensing Jesus (Wheaton, II: Crossway; 2012)
9.) St. Irenaeus of Lyon, c. 150 A.D.

REBELLION:
1.) C. S. Lewis, The Weight of Glory (HarperCollins Publishing Limited, 2013)
2.) Paul E. Miller, A Loving Life: In a World of Broken Relationships (Wheaton, II: Crossway, 2014)

GOSPEL:
1.) Abraham Kuyper (editor: Mr. James D. Bratt), Abraham Kuyper: A Centennial Reader (Wm. B. Eerdmans Publishing Co., 1998)
2.) Brennan Manning, The Furious Longing of God (Colorado Springs, CO: David C. Cook, 2009)
3.) Paul E. Miller, A Loving Life: In a World of Broken Relationships (Wheaton, II: Crossway, 2014)
4.) Drew Dyck, Yawning at Tigers (Nashville, TN: Thomas Nelson, 2014)
5.) Paul E. Miller, A Loving Life: In a World of Broken Relationships (Wheaton, II: Crossway, 2014)
6.) Lleonard Ravenhill, Lindale, TX, 1995
7.) St. Augustine, The Confessions of St. Augustine (Image Books ed edition, 1960)
8.) Logan Miller, Found in You (loganmillermusic.com)

RECREATION:
1.) C.S. Lewis, Mere Christianity (San Francisco: Harper, 1980)

FREDDY

In 2012, Freddy planted ekklesia, in the suburbs of St. Louis, with the desire to understand the every-day rhythms of the church. This exploration led to conversations on understanding family more deeply. As a former student pastor, family pastor, and now church planter, Freddy has a desire to rekindle an old conversation in new generations - to tell an old story. This is the story of Jesus, the story that shapes all stories. May this story be told in our homes for generations to come.

Freddy, his wife Michele, and two sons Ryder and Scout live in St. Charles, Missouri.

DAVID

David planted Mid-Cities Church in St. Louis, MO in 2014. He is passionate about seeing God's message of reconciliation bring about tangible transformation in both the hearts of people and the life of his city. As our hearts are connected with the Father's heart, the message of the gospel becomes clear and the work of Jesus becomes a reality. David is passionate about connecting those dots for others.

David, his wife Tara, his daughter Julia and son Moses live in Maplewood, Missouri.

also avaliable at storycatechism.com

Easter Catechism
Advent Catechism (coming soon)

Made in the USA
Lexington, KY
04 January 2016